CAGE
ELEVE

Best wishes

George Adams

For my mother and father

GERRY ADAMS

CAGE
ELEVEN

BRANDON

First published in 1990 by
Brandon Book Publishers Ltd
Dingle, Co. Kerry, Ireland.

British Library Cataloguing in Publication Data
Adams, Gerry
    Cage eleven.
    1. Northern Ireland. Suspected terrorists. Internment. –
    Biographies
    I. Title
    365.45092

    ISBN 0-86322-144-9

"Orange Drums, Tyrone, 1966" is reproduced from
Seamus Heaney's *North* by kind permission of Faber and
Faber Ltd.

Cover design by Robert Ballagh
Typeset by Seton Music Graphics Ltd, Cork
Printed by The Guernsey Press Co. Ltd, C.I.

BUÍOCHAS

I am indebted to Colette who never missed a visit and to Gearóid who has become my best literary critic. Thanks also to Danny D who did the illustrations for the original "Brownie" articles and who encouraged me to compile this collection; to Dáithí from Cage Ten who did the original typing; to Jim Gibney who read and advised on the first draft; to Robin and Thomas who helped and to Dave and Aengus who promised to help but didn't. Thanks also to Fionnuala who typed the first draft; to Mary Hughes and Sal (who got arrested in mid-sentence and is now in prison herself) who typed the final drafts; to big Eamonn and Pat who supervised photocopying and Deirdre who let them. Finally to the poet (who may have been Madra Rua but I can't recall) who composed "Ar an tslí go Béal Feirste"; to the late Ho Chi Minh whose poetry appears in "Nollaig Shona Dhaoibh"; to Seamus Heaney, whose verse is reproduced in "The Twelfth", and to anyone else I may have left out.

AR AN TSLÍ GO BÉAL FEIRSTE

I bhfad ar shiúl
Déanann soilse na Ceise
Breacadh bréagach
I spéir na hóiche.

Thar an Cheis Fhada
Ní gealtar aon lá
Chóiche.

Cé go lasann na mílte sóilse
Ann anocht,
Is siúd an áit is dorcha
In Éirinn –
Ó cheann ceann na hEorpa.

Roimh an dallrú úd
Stadtar
Mar ós cómhair réamh-chúirteanna
Ifrinn –

Aonrac,
Ineaglach,
Éadóchasach.

ON THE WAY TO BELFAST

From afar
The lights of Long Kesh
Make a false dawn
In the night sky.

But over Long Kesh
No dawn brightens
Ever.

Though a thousand lights blaze there
Tonight,
It is the darkest place
In Ireland –
In the whole of Europe.

Before that glare
One pauses –
As before the forecourts
Of hell –

Suddenly alone,
In dread
And despair.

CONTENTS

LONG KESH

Britain's Concentration Camp

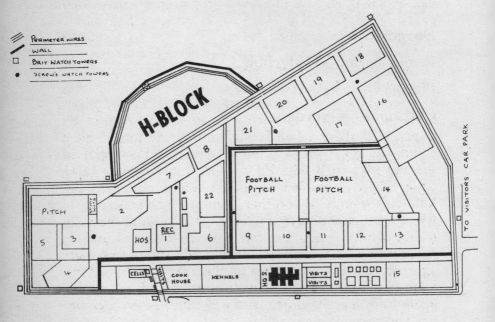

Long Kesh, Spring 1977. Cages 1 - 8 and 22 housed internees; the rest housed sentenced prisoners.

FOREWORD

Long Kesh concentration camp lies beside the M1
motorway about ten miles from Belfast and near the town
of Lisburn; nowadays the British government insists that
everyone should call it "Her Majesty's Prison, The Maze".
A rose by any other name . . .

Almost twenty years have passed since Long Kesh was
opened and through the years it has been a constant
element in the lives of all the members of my family . On
any one of the many days since then at least one of us has
been in there. My father was one of the first to be
imprisoned there when he and my Uncle Liam and a
couple of my cousins were interned without trial in
August 1971 in Belfast Prison and transferred to Long
Kesh when it opened to its unwilling guests in the
following month. My brother Dominic, who was only six
when our father was first interned, has been in the Kesh
for the last few years, and this year our Sean endured his
first prison Christmas. Our Liam did his time a few years
ago and Paddy A, our eldest brother, has been in and out
a few times. That's all the male members of our *clann* –
apart from me, of course, and a handful of brothers-in-
law and several more cousins.

Our female family members, like Colette and other
wives, sweethearts, sisters, sisters-in-law, aunts and my

11

mother, have spent almost twenty years visiting prisons. Yet for all that, ours is a perfectly normal family, and we are by no means unique. Long Kesh is full of our friends and the north of Ireland is coming down with families just like ours, all with a similar British penal experience.

Thousands of men and women have been incarcerated by the British government during this last twenty years. Thousands of wives and mothers and fathers and husbands and children have spent years visiting prisons, and it is they who do the real time. Today there are almost 800 Republican prisoners, most of whom are in British jails in the occupied six counties of Ireland. Others are imprisoned in Britain itself or are in the Dublin government's custody in Portlaoise and other prisons. A handful are in prisons in continental Europe or in the USA. Everyone in the nationalist community in the north of Ireland knows someone who is or has been in prison. None of us is immune.

I was first interned in March 1972 on the Maidstone, a British prison ship anchored in Belfast Lough. It was a stinking, cramped, unhealthy, brutal and oppressive floating sardine tin. We had the pleasure of forcing the British government to close it. A well publicized solid food strike, organized at an opportune time when the government was replacing its old Stormont parliament with an English cabinet minister, ensured the Maidstone's demise. We were airlifted to Long Kesh. A few months later I was released from Long Kesh, but thirteen months after that I was airlifted back in again, this time black and blue after being used as a punchbag in Springfield Road British Army barracks and spending a few days in Castlereagh interrogation centre.

Long Kesh had grown: now over twenty cages contained both internees and Loyalist and Republican sentenced prisoners. In the internment area I became the camp's most unsuccessful escapee, but I was consoled by my involvement in the successful elopements of many of my close comrades. I was only caught twice.

In October 1974 we showed our heartfelt appreciation for being interned without trial by joining the sentenced prisoners in burning down the camp, and just as it was being rebuilt my escape attempts caught up with me and I received two separate sentences of eighteen months and three years respectively. For a while I was an internee, a sentenced prisoner and a remand prisoner, all at the one time. Then I was moved with other would-be escapees to the sentenced area of the camp. From one cage to another – to Cage Eleven.

Today these cages no longer contain political prisoners, for they are held in Long Kesh's infamous H-Blocks and in other jails. Cage Eleven exists now only in the minds of those who were once crowded into its Nissen huts. It is a memory which reminds us, among other things, that the H-Blocks, like the British regime which spawned them, will one day be only a memory also.

The bulk of this book is derived from articles which were smuggled out of the cages and published, under the pen-name "Brownie", between August 1975 and February 1977 in *Republican News*, the Belfast republican newspaper which has since amalgamated to create *An Phoblacht/Republican News*. I was one of a small number of Long Kesh POWs who contributed to the weekly column in which we wrote, sometimes none too fluently, about a litany of issues as we perceived them from our barbed wire ivory tower.

Many of the pieces I wrote then and many of the chapters of this book are light-hearted, and the reader may imagine from them that Long Kesh was a happy, funny, enjoyable place. It was not then and it is not today. But the POWs were happy, funny, enjoyable people who made the best of their predicament. We wanted out but we did our whack as best we could. We did our time on each other's backs, and at times we may have got each other down but mostly we enjoyed one another's company and comradeship. The light-hearted pieces celebrate that enjoyment.

They also celebrate the lives of POWs who died in Long Kesh. Five men died while I was there. Another one died before I arrived and Henry Heaney passed away after my release. Henry, an old-age pensioner, had been sentenced to fifteen years under a law which makes it an offence just to have it in mind to do something. My abiding memory of Henry is of Sunday mornings before mass as he walked around Cage Twelve in his best suit. Henry was a great wee man and a sound Republican. Three years after his death, ten other sound Republicans were to die in the H-Blocks of Long Kesh. They died after five years of unprecedented prison protest by over 500 blanket-men and by women in Armagh in the heroic hunger strikes of 1981.

In this book the main characters are fictional, but they and their escapades are my way of representing life as it was in Long Kesh. Amongst those with whom I was privileged to share Cage Eleven were Bobby Sands, later MP for Fermanagh/South Tyrone and leader of the 1981 hunger strike; Danny "Dosser" Lennon, killed on IRA active service; Kevin "Dee" Delaney, killed in a separate IRA action; and Tommy "Todler" Tolan, killed by the fundraising wing of the Republican Clubs (now Workers Party) faction. There was Hugh Feeney, who endured 205 days of force-feeding in a prison in Britain along with Gerry Kelly and Dolours and Marion Price before the British government gave in to their demand for repatriation to jails in Ireland. There were Brendan "The Dark" Hughes and Brendan "Bik" McFarlane, later leaders in the H-Blocks blanket protests and hunger strikes; Bik was one of those who played a crucial role in the Great Escape of September 1983, the biggest jail-break in Europe since the Second World War, when thirty-eight POWs escaped from H7 in the H-Blocks.

These were some of Cage Eleven's residents. The rest of the men were equally remarkable; not so well known, but each unique in his own way. We did our time together, and this is my attempt to evoke, minus most of the f-ing and blinding, the atmosphere of that strange yet familiar world we shared. Sadly, some of the men who were there then are still in jail today. More of them, like Alec and Hugh, are only now being released. As I write another of my heroes, Terence "Cleaky" Clarke, is back in Long Kesh again, one of the many victims and scapegoats of a British mass trial. He was arrested months after the killing of two British soldiers who drove into mourners at Caoimhín Mac Brádaigh's funeral on the Andersonstown Road. Cleaky's only offence was that he was chief steward at Caoimhín's funeral. Big Sid is back too on a different charge. I hope that they, the many Irish POWs in jails everywhere, and the women in Maghaberry Prison and in jails in Britain recognize themselves and some of their prison experiences in the antics of the men of Cage Eleven. I hope, too, that for most of my readers this book is the closest they ever get to finding out what a prison camp or any other jail is really like.

Gerry Adams,
Belfast.

CAGE ELEVEN

I'm in bed at the moment, covered in breadcrumbs and skimpy grey British Army blankets, my knees tucked up under my chin and a blue plastic mug of blue plastic tea in my hand. The eejit in the next bed is doing his staunch Republican bit. "McSwiney taught us how to die," he is saying to his locker, and him only two weeks without a visit. The visits get cancelled regularly here. I think we are only entitled to one visit a month; the other three are "privileges" to be witheld as the Prison Governor decrees. After the first visitless week or so men take to their beds. It's not a pretty sight. Your Man has retired for the night already, pink pyjamas neatly creased and rosary beads in hand. And it's only seven o'clock.

During such phases the huts here are like some surrealistic limbo; made of corrugated tin sheets, they are unpainted Nissen huts. Leaky, draughty, cold, they are locked up at nine o'clock every night and unlocked at 7.30 every morning. We're inside them of course: us and our lines of bunk beds, lockers, our electric boiler, a kettle, a row of tables, a television set and a radio.

Somebody has just decided to brush the floor. Big floors in here, and thirty men lying, sitting, squatting, sprawled and splattered all over it. Nowadays there's thirty to a hut; it used to be worse. There are four or five

16

huts to a cage, depending on the size of the cage; two-and-a-half huts or three-and-a-half for living in; an empty hut for a canteen of sorts, and the other half-hut for "recreation", with a washroom and a "study" hut thrown in. Wired off with a couple of watch-towers planted around, and that's us.

Oh, and the drying hut. I can't forget that. The drying hut is where we hang our wet clothes. When we don't hang them on the wire. The drying hut is also the only place in here where you can be on your own. If nobody else is in it, that is.

All the gates open inwards. They probably do the same outside but you notice it more in here – that's called doing "bird". And everyone walks in an anti-clockwise direction. I don't know why. Internees do it, Loyalists do it as well. "Will you do a lap?" or "Fancy a boul?" or "Ar mhaith leat dul ag siúl?" and away you go around and around. And always against the clock. Maybe some instinct is at work. That's the funny thing about this place: a simple thing becomes a matter of life and death. I suppose it has always been like that. If you walk the other way you get the back ripped out of you.

Jail is unnatural. Even the men in this hut are wired up. Imagine thirty men of different ages, the oldest sixty-three, the youngest eighteen, all locked up together for years and years. I don't know how they stay in such good form. A well-informed comrade told me years ago that if he was building a sty for his pigs he could only keep twenty-odd pigs in a hut like this.

"Apart from the size," said he, "there isn't enough insulation and the walls must be breeze block or brick." Nowadays when he feels outraged at something or other he is heard to mutter: "This place isn't fit for pigs," but sure that's another story.

The floor is clean now and some of the boys are waiting for the late news. Sometimes we miss it and then there's a shouting match. Marooned as we are on the desert island of Long Kesh, television has become our electronic window on the world. The news programmes are of paramount importance. So is *Top of the Pops*; it has a consistently large audience while the audience for the news programmes go up and down depending on what's happening outside. News comes from other sources as well. From visits, from rumours. You would be surprised at the rumours which go the rounds here. *Scéal* is the word used to describe the widest possible generalised interpretation of the word "news". It includes real news as well as gossip, scandal, loose talk, rumour, speculation and prediction.

Much of it is manufactured by my friends Egbert, Cedric and Your Man. They do it almost by instinct now and the thing about it is that by the time it does the rounds here its source gets totally lost in the telling and retelling, the digesting and dissecting. What starts as an apparently innocent, throwaway remark from any of the aforementioned comrades soon becomes attributed to a BBC news-flash, an absolutely impeccable source on the IRA Army Council or a senior civil servant in the British Northern Ireland Office. And of course everyone adds their own wee bit; in fact, that's our main pastime. We manufacture it most of the time in our cage and some-times shout it across to other cages, or we talk at the wire when we are out of the cage for visits, football or other excursions. We also throw "pigeons" to each other. A pigeon is a well-tied snout (tobacco) tin containing a *scéal* note and a few pebbles for weight. We hurl our pigeons from cage to cage and thus have a line of communication which the screws can't penetrate. If you're a good thrower, that is.

The prison grub is awful. It comes to us from the "kitchens" in big containers on a lorry. At the cage gates the containers are transferred to a trolley; then whichever POWs are "on the grub" trundle the trolley across the yard and load the containers onto a "hot-plate" in the empty hut which poses as a canteen. If the food is particularly gruesome it will be refused by the Camp or the Cage Staff. If not, anyone who is "on the grub" serves it to whoever has the courage, constitution, or Oliver Twist appetite to digest it.

In the internment cages we rarely ate the prison grub, but then we were permitted to receive a fairly wide selection of cooked food which was sent in from outside by our families or friends. Here in the sentenced end the food parcels are more restricted and less frequent and so, alas, we have to eat the prison grub. At least some of the time. Apart from Seanna, that is, who eats it all the time. Sometimes we find more appropriate uses for certain alleged items of nutrition, and the cakes, which remain hard even with dollops of custard on them, came in handy on one occasion. During a British Army riot here we managed to keep them out of the cage for long enough by loosing volleys of gateaux at their ill-prepared ranks.

We usually dine together in food clicks – it took me years to establish that click is spelt clique. Some of our more ideologically correct comrades call them co-ops, and for a while the word commune was favoured by a few free spirits, but click is actually a more accurate description. A food click shares out its members' food parcels, usually on a rota basis, and divides the duties of cooking, plastic dish washing, tea making and so on in a similar fashion. Periodically someone drops out or is ejected from a food click. Occasionally others, for less quarrelsome reasons, go solo – known here as creating a "thirty-two county independent click" – but mostly collective eating predominates.

Cooking usually means reheating on the hot-plate, or on one of the ceiling heaters from the shower hut, removed and suitably adapted for the purpose, or even on a wee fire lit outside in a corner of the cage.

We drink loads of tea here. The Cage Eleven intelligentsia drink coffee. The water for both beverages is boiled in a communal boiler, which each hut has. Being "on the boiler" means being Gunga Dinn the water

19

carrier for a day. When I was in solitary once, I was able to make tea from a second-hand tea bag with water heated by placing a water-filled brown paper bag on the pipes. It took eighteen hours and was only tepid but it was still tea. I think. Without milk. Or sugar.

In between praising the food and manufacturing *scéal*, receiving *scéal*, discussing *scéal* and passing on *scéal*, we read a wee bit, back-stab each other a wee bit, talk a great deal and engage in a little sedition, which is mainly a matter of getting to understand the political situation which has us in here in Long Kesh. This process is occasionally revealing, sometimes amusing and always, next to *scéal*, the most time-consuming activity of most sane POWs. Other, less sane POWs make handicrafts but that's a habit I've avoided so I can't really comment on it. A lapsed handicrafter told me once of his belief that the making of harps, Celtic crosses, purses, handbags and even soft toys was addictive. Painting hankies with coloured marker pens was, he believed, less serious – merely a phase all POWs go through.

We also go through phases of depression – the big D. On the outside marriages break up, parents die, children get sick; all normal worries intruding into our impotent abnormality. Some comrades have nervous breakdowns. Some do heavy whack. Comrades also die in here through lack of medical facilities and in one case a British Army bullet, and people are dying outside all the time as the war goes on. It all has its effects in this bastard of a place. That's one thing POWs have in common: we all hate Long Kesh. But we try not to let it get us down.

Some POWs sing or play musical instruments which is one of the reasons why others try to escape. Would-be escapees cause the prison administration a great deal of anxiety, but the prison administration doesn't like being anxious. So to relieve the prison regime's anxiety we are forced to endure British military raids when, at an unearthly hour in the morning and entirely without notice, a British Colonel Blimp makes a commando-style raid into our huts and orders us to "put your hands on your blankets, look at the ceiling, then when told to do so you will get dressed and take your knife, fork and spoon to the canteen". Just to show he's serious he is accompanied by a few regiments of combat troops. Why we're told to bring our knives, forks and spoons I'll never know. We never get fed. Sometimes they tell us we can take our "treasures" with us; I've never been able to understand that either. Sometimes they spreadeagle us on the wire and sometimes they beat us. They always make a mess of the place.

As you can see from all this, the prison administration takes its anxiety very seriously, which is more than can be said for most of the rest of us. They tried to give us prison numbers, taking away our names and calling us prisoner 747611 or prisoner 726932. But we refused to use our numbers and now the screws have given up using them too. After all, we're only here because of bad luck, stupidity, miscarriages of justice, being in the wrong place at the wrong time. And, of course, because our respective parents conceived us in or near that part of north-east Ireland which is under British occupation, at a time when we were assured of reaching imprisonable age just when some citizens of this state decided they had had enough of it. And once we were here in Long Kesh, like Topsy we just growed and growed.

Sometimes we give ourselves a hard time. As Your Man says in his wounded way, "Are the men behind the wire behind the men behind the wire?" But mostly we save up our resentments for the prison administration. We mess up head counts, make hurling sticks out of prison timber, protest regularly, organize our own structures, read books they don't understand, ignore their instructions, try to escape, succeed in escaping. Generally we just do our own thing. We enjoy political status in Cage Eleven . We would do all of the above anyway even if we didn't have political status. In fact we would probably do worse, but for now we co-exist in our strange little barbed-wire world, enduring a unique experience under and because of the unique political apartheid which exists in this little British colony in the top right-hand corner of Ireland.

Your Man says we'll all be out by April 24 next year. I don't know about you but I wouldn't believe a word of it. How would he know anyway? He's a bit of a hallion. Maybe his brother told him. His brother's best friend is married into a family which has a son who is engaged to a woman whose father works for a man who is very thick with some old chap who works as a civil servant at the British Home Office in London. And he would know, wouldn't he?

April 24. Let me see. That's a Monday. Funny now, that being a Monday. Your Man wouldn't be quick enough to figure out that for himself. You see, Monday's a good release day. Now if it had been a Sunday, well then you could say for certain Your Man was lying. But it's not so easy now, is it? I wonder if Egbert or Cedric know anything about this. Egbert knows Your Man's brother pretty well. I think I'll go and suss him out.

"Ah. Egbert. Just the man I'm looking for. Did you hear about the letter from the British Home Office? About releases in April? You did? What do you mean there's a copy of it on the wall in the Governor's office? Egbert, c'mon. Give us a bit of *scéal*."

Only one hour, four minutes and one thousand and six hundred and twenty-four days to go.

EARLY RISERS

"At least I'm not in for stealing," Your Man said.

"Not this time anyway," I replied, as I left him steeping his feet in the jawbox. Things aren't going too well between us this last wee while. Him and his early rises!

There are two main groups in here. I'm not talking about left-wingers or right-wingers, about hawks or doves, nor about this issue or that issue. The truth of the matter is simple and straightforward. There's Us, and there's the Early Risers. That mightn't seem much of an issue to anyone who hasn't been here but, nevertheless, it is a rather complex problem. To begin with, why would anyone in a place like Long Kesh want to get up at half past seven in the morning?

Why indeed? Nobody knows! Nobody, that is, except the Early Risers themselves. And when you ask one of them they grin and yawn and say,

"Ach, sure it's a good morning," or

"I always used to get up early;" or even

"I do a bit of training."

It does seem a bit far-fetched, doesn't it? And the way they do it! All carefully arranged and co-ordinated the night before. Jimmy wakes Jackie who shakes Alfie who rouses Cecil who kicks Alphonsus and away they go, creeping half-naked into the dawn. Hut by hut, cage by cage they muster. In the washrooms, by the tea-boilers and under the showers. When everyone else is being dragged out of bed by ambitious or power-crazy Hut OCs the Early Risers are sitting, smiling their superior smiles and trying to look innocent, just as if they hadn't been doing anything at all.

"Good morning . . . Maidin mhaith . . . Did you finally make it?" Grins, smiles and smirks cloak the back-stab: "Morning John" (*You waster*); "Dia dhuit Seamus" (*A amadán bhocht*).

At one stage the Cage OC feared a coup d'etat was being hatched in the wee small hours and so the IO was put to work. I should explain that the IO is the Intelligence Officer. The OC is the Officer-in-Charge. Very formal and militaristic, but that's the way prison camp is. We elect an OC and he selects a staff and that includes an adjutant, an IO, a quartermaster and various other dignatories. I digress. Back to the Early Risers. As I was saying, the IO was put to work to check them out. Nothing transpired, however, as the IO (known ever since as "Mattress-Back") kept watch from a horizontal position, and that, as all well-bred subversives know, is no way to do intelligence work — unless you're Mata Hari, of course, which needless to say Mattress-Back isn't, worse luck.

Anyway, not only do the Early Risers get up early, they also go to bed early. And Us? Well, we like to watch TV or listen to records, or sing and shout and generally tire ourselves out before getting into the cart. Which is only sensible; like, it's no good going to bed unless you're sleepy — anyone can see the logic in that. Anyone, that is, except the Early Risers! *They* think we do it deliberately to keep them awake. Regardless of all their complaints, though, they still manage to get up early the next morning, which just goes to prove my point: whatever it is they're up to must be very important indeed. I'm back to where I started — back to Your Man. Now he's gone and joined the Early Risers!

I only found out about it the other week. It was one of those lovely mornings for lying on but the screw had great difficulty in unlocking the door and he woke everyone in the process. They lock us up at night, you know; you would think it was deliberate. But anyway, having locked us up at night they have then to unlock us in the morning — at half past seven. When anyone with a bit of sense is well covered up and cosy. The morning I'm telling you about, the rattle of the keys woke me, and just as I was slipping back into a semi-coma I thought I saw Your Man creeping up the hut. "Ha Ha," I thought to myself, "Nature calls early . . ."

However, on being kicked out of bed myself, at a much more respectable hour, I saw that Your Man was still up and that he was behaving exactly like the others.

"I've started learning Irish," he explained. "And I study in the morning when it's quiet."

He must think I'm a complete eejit. Learning Irish, he says. He doesn't know "Cad é mar atá tú" from "Bórd na Móna". Not that I've anything against the Irish; I'm learning it myself. Only it's very hard in here. It's difficult to find the time to do everything.

Maybe I should go to bed early tonight after all. What a waste it is to be spending these good mornings in bed. Not that Your Man has anything to do with me thinking of getting up early. Not on your life! He definitely must have a move on but sure if he wants to keep it to himself, well, I have more important things to worry about than the behaviour of a latchico like him. I've got a visit, and if I'm up early I'll be able to do a wee bit of training and have a good shower before the rest of the lads get up. I only hope I can get to sleep early — some of the blirts here would act the eejit all night. And I must get someone to wake me. Maybe I'll be able to do an extra wee bit of Irish as well. And maybe Your Man will tell me what he's working on!

SCREWS

I hobbled to the doctor's during the week. Luckily I had been able to time the spraining of my ankle to coincide with the weekday hours in which the prison regime allocates a doctor for the thousand or so prisoners here. I was feeling pretty pleased with myself because if you are going to sprain your ankle (or anything else for that matter) in Long Kesh there's nothing like getting the time right. Timing is everything. If you make a mess of that you could die waiting for the doctor to come. On the other hand, if you're perfectly healthy it's pretty good *craic* going to see the doctor here. For one thing, it gets you out of the cage.

First stop is the cage gate. It opens into a wee wire tunnel. That's where the screws rub you down. Out of the tunnel (the regime calls it an air-lock) then out, via the other cage gate. A brisk hobble takes us to the wicker gate in the wall which now surrounds our cages. All movement of prisoners is recorded at each gate. Passage through all gates is accompanied by your screw shouting "one on" or "one off" depending on whether you're leaving or arriving. The screw on gate duty then makes his mark in a little ledger, denoting your departure from or arrival into the area controlled by his gate. All very elementary. Three gates within yards of each other with screws at each one. Big screws, wee screws, strong screws, weak screws. Screws of all shapes and sizes: smart, clean, regimental screws; washed-out, bogging, scruffy screws. Security screws, visit screws, sports screws, friendly screws and nasty screws. Screws performing all kinds of functions, every role programmed to suit their capabilities. Every role programmed to subvert our attitudes.

Beyond the wall now and on to the road which runs alongside the visiting boxes. Lots of muck about the place. Building workers escorted by screws, sentry-boxes inhabited by screws; screws in vans, screws at gates, screws to-ing and fro-ing – all programmed, all functioning well. When I feel fit enough to go to the doctor's I have my own special screw to keep me company. He is a remarkable piece of humankind – a right pockel. I pause, he pauses; I hobble fast, he hobbles fast; I stop, he stops. I smirk at him, he smiles shyly back; I glare at him, he looks away; I address him as "my good man", he grins stupidly; I ignore him, he observes me sleekitly. I go to the doctor's, he goes to the doctor's.

I think he really hates me. Deep inside his blue uniform, I reckon he really, really harbours a burning hatred for me. Like, I'm not sure of that, of course, but the majority of screws here behave, most of the time, as if they hate the prisoners.

Just me and him then. Almost at the doctor's. Brit watch-towers within range, more building workers, the whole place being assembled on grip-work and overtime. Out of the ashes of Long Kesh arose the Maze Prison. Only one more box and one more gate to go. Only one more screw to pass: this one is programmed to open and close gates and to write down names. A breakthrough in time and motion. Usually they train two screws for complicated performances like that. One to open gates, one to do the names. This looks like an experiment, something like the one-man buses when they came out at first. Inside another cage now, my screw following closely. I'm glad we both made it. I tell him this and ask him, in my most regal tone, to open the door. He scurries forward, fumbles, gets embarrassed, succeeds. I ignore him and we step inside, me into a partitioned "waiting room", he into a corner.

No one else about. I examine the graffiti: "P.J. Can we ask for a retrial?", "Wee Arthur, 15 years! Wait for me Sadie I love you", "6 into 32 won't go", "This place is hereby renamed Lourdes – if you get cured here it'll be a miracle", "Bump", "Jim O'Toole, 12 years", "Mickey" ... a whole wall of them. An interesting but unprintable one on the window-sill. Another one about that much-maligned old Italian Republican, Red Socks himself. The place is pigging. I sit down. My screw looks away again. A young lad comes in: a skinhead haircut, tattoos across his knuckles. He's a YP – a young prisoner. There is a swelling below his left eye, a bruise on his forehead. He sits down, ill at ease; I grin at him, ignoring the screws, and offer him a cigarette. He takes two drags while the screw has his back turned and then hands it back to me. The poor kid is frightened to death. He still hasn't spoken a word.

"Do you want some snout?" I ask. I give him another drag and wait for his answer, feeling protective, disdainful of the screws.

Suddenly he leans across to me: "Can you get a complaint made about a screw?"

"Aye, I'll get our OC to see the Governor."

"It's about _____. He beat me up. He beats all of us up." His words rush at me in a frenzied whisper. He hesitates, then, " _____ is a bastard. He beats us up all the time. He's the worst screw of the lot."

The screws at the door must know what he's telling me. They must know what's happening. They pretend they don't. They ignore us. The YP gets cockier and pockets the cigarettes I give him. He is about fifteen or sixteen, pale-faced bar the bruising. I ask him for his name. He gives me his surname. He looks uncomfortable again as I leave. I hear the screws say something. I go into the doctor's.

More screws – three of them in white coats. Clean screws called medics. We examine my leg together. I wince, they wince; I explain how it happened, they nod their heads sympathetically. The doctor prescribes something or other. The screw with the pen calls me mister. I wonder how they will deal with the YP. I consider telling the doctor about him, just to get rid of my frustrations, just to get shouting a bit. Then I look at them all and I feel lost for a second. They know there is something wrong: they're programmed for that eventuality. They move away and I go out. Past the YP. He pretends he doesn't see me. Past the screws, who look sheepish. My own personal screw tags along behind me and we hobble back. Back past the gates, across the road. When my screw slips in the muck I mutter "idiot" at him.

I notice heavy cable beside the wicker gate: they must be going to make it automatic. I pass more screws. We head for the cage, but I hobble past our cage towards the next one. My screw follows uncomplainingly. I talk with our Camp OC at the wire, giving him a rundown on the YP's complaint. Afterwards my screw and I part company at our cage gate. I ignore him. He says goodbye. He uses my first name. I come through the gates, in by the tunnel. Through the next gate and across the yard. He heads off towards the gate in the wall.

Inside the hut I drink my tea. Outside the huts the screws continue their patrols. Outside our cages they hunch against the wind. At their gates they jangle keys. In sentry-boxes they huddle against the cold. Don't ask me why they do it. I'm not programmed like they are so I couldn't give you an answer. It took the British Army, the RUC, a British judge and a few Special Branch men to get me in here. Screws serve their sentences voluntarily.

Well, they do so for a lucrative wage plus overtime. I don't really hate them. I'm not so much against anything or anybody, it's just that I'm for a lot of things. None of them include screws.

But then nobody here likes screws. No one likes thinking of Paddy Teer dead in the prison "hospital". Teddy Campbell dying his last few years here to be released to a premature grave. Jim Moyna breathing his last agonizing breath as he fought to keep living against all the wire, all the screws and all the gates between his cage and the doctor's. Frankie Dodds dying at the gate of the cage – just outside the wire tunnel.

My personal screw whined when I called him an idiot. He is programmed to do that. If he had me on my own in solitary I couldn't say that or if I did he wouldn't whine – not while he had assistance. That's the way screws are programmed.

And now here in Long Kesh the screws are being programmed to take political status off us. But they know and we know it won't be an easy job. The H-Blocks will be their Waterloo. The ones like _____ who beats up YPs don't understand. But then they never do. That's why they're screws. They're not all like that, of course; some of them are decent enough; but most of them aren't.

They are out there now, outside this hut, hunched against the wind, huddled against the cold. They are out there, outside this window watching in, jangling their keys. They are out there now, they and the British Army, keeping us in here. For the time being anyway.

CRATUR

He was from somewhere near the Border and he got his name from his habit of addressing everyone as "cratur". He rarely volunteered conversation but, on request, would say, "Sin sin, cratur", (That's that, cratur) or perhaps, "Okay, cratur". He was a man of amicable disposition but, because of his aloofness, Cratur didn't make many firm friends. Everyone treated him with respect and some with caution; others didn't treat with him at all.

On one occasion, having offered to clean out the drying hut, he did not content himself with merely cleaning and tidying. Instead he gathered every last item of clothing that had been deposited there since the introduction of internment in August 1971 and expelled them from the hut. And he didn't just deposit them outside the hut but carried them out to the gate fence and flung them over. Some snagged on the German razor wire where they flapped colourfully in the breeze; others lay in a large pile in no-man's-land, all now inaccessible to their owners. The Cage OC, besieged by POWs complaining about their losses of favourite shirts, pullovers, Y-fronts and even socks, demanded an explanation.

"Why did you do that?" he growled at Cratur.

"Ach, sin sin, cratur," came the reply. Agus sin mar a bhí sé. (And that's how it was.)

31

Uneventful days passed – uneventful, that is, by Lazy K standards. Of course, the odd complaint about this and that did the rounds, but only when the Great Sunday Paper Scandal came to light did things get serious again. In the study hut the Cage Staff deliberated their next move.

"As I see it," said the very short-sighted Cage Adjutant, "We have not got one Sunday paper today; the screws are holding them. They are probably sitting reading them now. OC, I propose that we take militant action, OC." Now you know why he was Adjutant.

"OC," he crawled, "I propose we stop the visits."

"We don't get visits on Sundays," interjected the Cage Intelligence Officer whose duty it was to have information like this. "And, furthermore, the screws have told me that the papers did come in today."

"And who, may I ask, received them?" asked the Adjutant, knowing full well that he could ask what he wanted.

"Cratur got them," replied the IO, proudly victorious in the verbal battle.

And as it was said, so it was also revealed – *Sunday Newse*s and *Sunday World*s, *Sunday Presse*s and *Sunday Independent*s could plainly be seen sticking out from under Cratur's mattress, while supplements and reviews peeked coyly from beneath his pillow.

"What are you doing with those?" screamed the OC.

"Ach, sin sin, cratur," came the smiling reply from atop the mountain of newsprint. Agus sin mar a bhí sé.

And then the Brits came in. Half past five one cold morning. "This is a military raid! Put your hands on your heads. Look at the ceiling!" barked the uniformed English accent. "You will get dressed! One at a time! And stand at the wire! Do not move until you are told!" And so, sleep-befuddled Brit lunatics in uniforms threatened, ordered and cajoled even more sleep-befuddled Irish lunatics in underpants out into the cold night.

"I'm not standing at the wire," said Cratur to a forty-five-year-old private.

"Oh yes you are, you Irish . . ."

"Nawh, I'm not," said Cratur. "I've got a bad heart and I'll faint in this cold."

"Get that man against the wire!" screamed a tall, thin, Sandhurst accent.

"Right Sir," said a corporal as he fell beneath the full sixteen stone, ten pounds of fainting Cratur.

"Okay," said the medic, "put him back to bed."

We all took turns cleaning out the huts. It was called being on the floor.

"You're on the floor in the morning."

"Right, cratur," said our friend.

"Lights out now lads."

The hut slipped into sleep, beds creaking as men moved restlessly in the night. The wind wailed its way through the wire, screws patrolled their mercenary beats. All was as usual. Then a mop bucket clanked and the sound of running water washed away the silence. Splash. And a gallon of water cascaded up the hut. Splash. Splash. And splash again.

Roused out of his bed, the Hut OC swam towards Cratur. "What the hell are you doing, you half-baked eejit!" he choked.

"I'm washing out the hut, cratur," came the reply, and the OC went down under a tidal wave which swept through the hut. "Ach, sin sin," said Cratur as he waded back to bed.

Months and months later and still things got no better. Cratur "sin sinned" his way over, under, by, through and on top of cage regulations. Never did he break a rule: always he carried it out to the letter. A careless order to "put the bins out of the cage," was met with bins being flung over wires and gates. "Brushing out the hut" meant mangled bodies caught unawares amid milk cartons and bed-fluff. Brit Military Police were soaked with holy water on one raid, prisoners were almost killed on another. And yet everyone liked Cratur. He was the exception and his notoriety was secretly welcomed by his comrades.

"You would think they'd let him out, wouldn't you?" we said to one another. "He's dead sound, only they shouldn't keep him here." But they did. Not that Cratur cared. He grinned and scared screws.

"You can't do that," declared a stern-faced, pimple-ravished Governor.

"Ach, I can cratur." And he did and grinned as he did so.

"You're the Devil," said Cratur one morning to a young man of impeccable background. "You with your black beard and dark face. You're the Devil," he snorted as he hurried from the hut.

"What will I do?" pleaded the accused.

"Ach," said the OC, "It will be okay. Cratur never did anybody any harm. You'll be okay."

But he wasn't. That night he awoke to find a tall, bulky figure in priest's vestments at the foot of his bed. "Begone Satan!" intoned the priest's vestments in a country brogue, "Begone! Begone!"

"Mommy!" cried the condemned and helpless victim. "Help. For God's sake, somebody help!"

And the priest's vestments sighed. "Sin sin," they sighed and slid away, leaving the exhausted and exorcised child to change his soiled bedsheets.

And then, one morning *scéal* had it that Cratur was being moved to Muckamore Mental Home or some place like that. Everyone was sorry and sad to see him go. Comrades, exorcised and bedevilled alike, came to bid him farewell.

"It's the best thing really, you know," they said to one another. "This place wasn't doing him any good at all. But still, I'm sorry to see him leaving."

"All the best," they yelled.

"Ach, sin sin, cratur," came the reply, and away Cratur went.

"I feel cat about that," said a usually hardened RTP (Rough Tough Provie). "I don't like him going into a home, it's a pity on the poor man. Sure, he wouldn't do anybody any harm."

And RTPs and screws for once agreed that it was a bad job and, having agreed, they went their separate ways.

And Cratur went his. "Sin sin," he said.

And "Sin sin, cratur," whispered the shadowy figure to himself as he slid noiselessly through the open window of the mental hospital later that night.

"Could I have a pint of stout please, and a wee one," he asked as he hoisted himself onto a bar-stool in Dundalk the following day. "Sin sin, cratur," he chuckled into the telephone, "I know I can't talk to the Camp Kommandant himself. Just give him a message, will you? Tell him it's long distance and just say 'Sin sin, cratur'. He'll know what you mean."

And a few customers smiled to themselves at the tall, bulky figure who stood that night, pint in hand, singing "The Men Behind The Wire". And he smiled back at them and winked. "Sin sin," he grinned. "Sin sin, cratur."

Agus sin mar a bhí sé.

THE FIRE

"It's so cold, if this was school we'd be sent home," Your Man muttered.

"I know," Cedric shivered, "I'm foundered."

"Youse two should be well hopped up," Egbert scolded. He wore a blanket poncho-style over his anorak and his jeans were thrust into knee-high football socks. His head was encased in one of Cleaky's balaclavas and he had football socks also on each hand. He lay on top of his bunk.

"In winter weather you have to wear winter clothes," he observed.

"The last time I saw you dressed up like that you had just burned down the camp," Your Man said.

"It was not I," Egbert protested with a smile, "I was but an innocent at large, wandering along life's busy highway ..."

"You're in quare form anyway," Cedric interrupted. "It makes a welcome change."

"It must have been a good visit."

"'Twas, 'twas, 'pon my soul it was," Egbert agreed, "'tis wonderful the things the love of my life can do beneath a poncho."

"Aye, dead on! But you didn't go out on a visit like that did you?" Your Man asked.

"'Course I did. It was as sound as a bell. And Angela said the same as you."

"What was that?"

"That the last time I was dressed like this was after the fire."

"It was just about this time last year," Cedric said. "Remember?"

"I'll never forget it," said Your Man with feeling. "It was the 15th of October. I was never so scared in my life. It was desperate."

"Ah, but you were a poor wee internee. Up in the sentenced end we never flinched," Egbert boasted.

"Houl' on, I don't know about that," Cedric protested.

"We were ready for battle," Egbert continued.

"Aye, bottle or draught," Your Man interrupted. "If it wasn't for the internees you'd be banjaxed. We provided the brains."

"I don't know about that either." Cedric was adamant.

"What do you know?" they both exclaimed.

"I know as much as you two anyway. I kept a diary. I still have it. I had it on me during the fire and the fighting, then I dumped it when the Brits overran us. I smuggled a copy out afterwards but if you want to read the original I'll get it for youse, so I will. I've it dumped away in a handy place."

"Okay," the others agreed, "that would be interesting."

"Right," said Cedric. "I won't be long."

He returned a few minutes later with a small packet wrapped in polythene. He unfolded his bundle carefully and passed a handful of soiled and creased pages to Egbert.

"They're stinking!" Egbert protested, "I thought you said it was a diary!"

"I hid them in a sewer. That's why I still have them. They were too smelly to send out. And they are a diary," Cedric affirmed. "Look!"

He took the pages from Egbert and spread them on the floor. His audience leaned over and read intently.

Saturday October 12:
Nearly six weeks now without food except for a half pint of milk and three rounds of bread daily. We have been refusing the prison food because after numerous representations by our staff to the prison regime the food continued to disimprove so we protested by dumping it over the wire. The prison regime retaliated by stopping our food parcels. We are also draping bed-linen on the cage wire in protest at the lack of clean sheets. Clean linen is supplied very irregularly, sometimes every six weeks. These protests have settled into an easy-going pattern. Everyone is in good form. The biggest excitement was when we discovered a dozen rounds of mouldy bread in wee Harry's locker. He couldn't eat it without butter, he said.

Sunday October 13:
Things may be building up to a head. There was a meeting between the various OCs today. Months ago they presented a list of all the main points of contention to the Prison Governor. These included food, laundry, general living conditions, education facilities (or the lack of them) and the treatment of remand prisoners. It was when the prison administration refused to move on any of these that the present protests started. Today there is scéal about a major build-up of British troops around the visiting area. This is why I'm speculating that things may be coming to a head. Some time ago, after particularly vicious beatings on a Brit raid, our staff warned that if the British Army came into the cages to beat or baton men then we would burn the camp to the ground. Some men sent their clothes and other effects out with their visitors this afternoon.

Monday October 14:
Semaphore is being used to signal messages between the internees' cages and the sentenced end of the camp. There is also a lobby building up, especially among our escape fanatics, that there should be no burning unless accompanied by a major escape. In our cage Your Man is arguing that as long as the perimeter is secure the British government will be unaffected, except in the short-term, by the camp being burned. He argues

that burning the camp has no more potential than merely publicizing for a few weeks the conditions in here. But a mass escape under cover of the fire, aimed at putting hundreds of men outside – either through tunnels or by storming gates or the perimeter – would advance the entire struggle, he says.

More men sent their clothes out today.

Tuesday October 15:
It's now really the 19th October and I'm writing this in a little makeshift shelter of blackened, sooty, corrugated tin. The huts in our cage are no more. They disappeared in what has come to be the most unusual and dramatic days of my young life. The trouble started on Tuesday in Cage Thirteen. A screw made derogatory and sexual remarks about some lad's wife. The OC of the cage asked that the screw be removed from the cage. This is a long-standing arrangement between our staff and the prison regime. Our people have never abused it and the ordinary screws and SOs willingly work this procedure. It cuts down on any real aggro between them and the POWs. It has always suited us both. This time the senior screws (probably on orders) refused to comply with Cage Thirteen's OC's request to remove the offending screw. Reinforcements were put into the cage. There were scuffles. Our lads put all the screws out of the cage. The Prison Governor then arrived. He insisted that the POWs involved should come forward and go voluntarily to the punishment block. This was another breach of a long-standing and mutually beneficial arrangement whereby our Camp OC would usually be brought to the cage involved, to direct if neccesary the men to the cells. The Prison Governor ordered that this was not to happen on this occasion. He warned that if the men did not come forward the British Army would come in and forcibly remove them. When the Camp OC heard of this he sent word to the Governor reminding him of the republican commitment to burn the camp if the British Army were used. He asked that the matter be deferred until the following morning to allow things to cool down. It was almost lock-up. The Governor refused that request. The OC then asked permission to go to Cage Thirteen. The Governor refused that

request also: he ordered all screws out of the sentenced cages. They withdrew without any interference from our lads. The Camp OC then sent word again to the Governor that if the British Army were brought in the camp would burn. He got word back that the Governor was no longer in charge. The British Army was in control.

Down here in the internee end we knew nothing of all this. I only picked up the scéal afterwards. Funnily enough I was at a cage staff-meeting to discuss Your Man's idea about coupling any future burning to an escape. The OC of the internees had earlier agreed to an informal request to put this idea to the Camp OC up at the sentenced end. Your Man was just doubling up by formalizing his request. We had just agreed to do just this after a good discussion when someone burst into the half-hut where we were meeting and told us he thought the sentenced end was burning. When we rushed outside a single black plume of smoke was ascending heavenwards up at the top end of the camp. Our Cage OC rushed up to the wire to be told "Burn it all!" by the OC of the internees. So we burned it.

Me and Your Man and Todler were the last three out of our cage. All the internees were to assemble over at Cage Four. Our Cage OC led the men over and we three were delegated to check that no one was left behind. As we went around, all the huts were well ablaze. It was a bit eerie. Kathleen Thompson had sent me in a Kris Kristofferson LP. Someone must have been playing it when the trouble started because amidst all the confusion and smoke and flames "Bobby Magee" was blasting out, and going slower and slower as the heat reached it. That will be one of my abiding memories of the Long Kesh fire. When we left the cage the screws were already formed up across the big space between the cages to prevent us joining up with the sentenced end. The screws were assembled down at the visits. At first I thought they were peelers. Maybe they were. There were none of our lads near us as we three cut across. It was scary. The cage lights were smashed but the screws saw us in the big searchlights. They fired rubber bullets and gas. The gas was definitely CR gas. Not CS. I know the taste of CS. I swallowed some of the CR. It's difficult to describe the sensation. It's like choking on balloons which inflate to fill out and smother your windpipe and your lungs. I remember thinking this must be what it's like to drown.

When our cage assembled one man, a Derryman, was missing. Some of us went off and found him. I don't know how. He had got lost in all the noise and confusion. His nerves were gone.

Things were hectic for a wee while. Apparently, though none of us knew this, the idea was to try and join up with the sentenced men. Some internee cages had managed to do just that before the screws (or the peelers) cut off the only adjoining road – the Yellow Brick Road as Johnsie calls it – and our staff was trying to decide what to do. Everyone had burned their own cages and we were all milling about. Your Man volunteered to organize things while the staff sorted out their options. Very quickly he formed us all up – and there were a few hundred of us – into ranks. He drilled us for a few minutes until order was restored then we sent our wee foraging squads out to burn places outside the cages. The screws (or peelers) didn't really interfere. Only when we tried to penetrate or breach their lines did they get aggressive. Otherwise they just fired rubber bullets at our burning-squads. It appeared that their orders were to contain us within the camp – or within our part of the camp. They fired CR gas continuously for the first few hours.

When everything burnable was burning we just sat back and admired our handiwork. By this time Your Man's voice had expired so the Hurdy Gurdy man had to act as his megaphone. Three things happened to me. I discovered the Heathen wrapped in a blanket (probably the only POW in the camp with a blanket) and beneath it he was hugging a big mess-tin of sausages. (He gave me one.) God knows where he got them. Then I bumped into Dickie Glen and said to him that I'd love a smoke. He went off and in a few minutes came back and presented me with a Hamlet cigar. God alone knows where he got it. The last thing was when I was helping John Joe McGirl and I asked him if he was all right. "If you're all right, I'm all right," he answered. His jaw had been broken by a rubber bullet.

41

Wednesday October 16:
After a while we put out scouts to warn of any counter-attacks
and we retired into Cage Four. The wounded and the older men
were put into what remained of one hut and the rest of us sat
about smoking and talking. It was impossible to describe the
scene. The whole night and the skyscape was blazing. Every so
often a watchtower would topple over and collapse in a great
fanfare of sparks and flames. There were fairly loud explosions
going off all over the place. Eventually we located them as
exploding Kosangas containers. Occasionally a rubber bullet or
gas grenade popped. All the time helicopters with searchlights
circled overhead. Occasionally they dropped gas-bombs.

As dawn slowly eased itself awake the OC of internees told
us all to sit in the centre of the cage. He was expecting the
British Army to come in at first light. He was going to seek a
commitment that no one would be ill-treated. As the night
lightened into morning I looked around at Big Ted. He and I
had been sitting back to back, keeping each other in an upright
position. Beneath his beard and all the grime and soot and dirt
his face was grey. So was everyone else's. I remember thinking
to myself that mine must be the same colour. It suited our
environment. Everything around us was in shades of grey:
grey wire, ash-grey smouldering debris, soot-blackened timber,
charred wooden beams, tar-black tarmac, grey clouded sky, and
hundreds of grey-faced men sitting and squatting amidst it all.

Then the Brits came in. They came squealing and whooping.
Psychological, I suppose. We remained silent. That had its psy-
chological effect also. It silenced them. Soon they stood silently
outside our cage, facing us. I noticed that they were also grey.
An officer with a megaphone instructed us all to get to our feet.
None of us moved; we just sat there silently staring at them.
Waiting. Then our OC went forward. He sought assurances of
good conduct and asked for the wounded to be taken away. The
Brits wanted to ascertain immediately that a certain two
internees were not missing; they wanted them brought forward.
Our OC refused. Eventually an arrangement was negotiated:
the wounded would be taken away; the rest of our men would be

paraded by our own staff for identification by screws, and then we would go back to our original cages. All of this would be supervized by screws. The British Army would do an initial body frisk and then theirs would be a watching brief.

When the negotiations were concluded Harry F paraded us, and as we stood to attention he explained to us what was happening. He did a great job that morning. He made a wee speech and then we moved away from the centre of the cage and made room for the British Army. As they filled our space their officer demanded that the two internees he was seeking come forward. Harry F told him again that none of us were being taken away. He suggested that he would escort a screw to where the two men were, and this was done. It was no big deal: the Brits only wanted to check that the two hadn't escaped. As soon as this became known our lads relaxed. Before this the fittest and best of the internees had grouped around the two wanted men. Now some of the lads started wisecracking, challenging individual British soldiers to step outside and all the usual tomfoolery.

Things got a bit hairy again when we were ordered against the wire for a body-search. No one moved. One of our staff sorted it out by stepping forward and instructing us to go to the wire. We were there for a good while. Nothing unexpected occurred. Sly digs and the odd knee or kick between the legs, but nothing that equalled razing Long Kesh. We were IDed by a senior screw accompanied by a senior member of our staff. As we walked back to our original cages we became aware of the popping of rubber bullets and gas grenades from the top end of the camp. As I went back into Cage Two this eased off. All was quiet. The Brits were still everywhere.

When Your Man came into the cage he winked at me and pulled a pair of two-foot-long bolt-cutters from where he had them hidden down the leg of his denims. At about 8.30 the main Brit force pulled back, though sizeable squads were deployed in strategic positions and foot patrols still made their way continuously up and down through the debris. About ten o'clock we lined up to get a carton of milk and two rounds of bread. Later the internees who had made it up to the sentenced *end were escorted back in a long crocodile of bloodied, grinning men sandwiched between rows of heavily-armed British soldiers. All marching down the Yellow Brick Road. At one o'clock we were given one blanket each, head-counted and then, lying where we stood, we slept.*

Thursday October 17:
All day we heard of the battle of the football pitch up at the sentenced end. By all accounts it was intense, with the POWs giving as good as they got. There were two major battles at the gates of the football pitch. The lads captured one Brit and the helicopter bombed them with scores of gas grenades. In fact, the Brits started their attack with an air assault but, despite this, the boys held on. When the Brits eventually subdued them, after being repulsed a number of times, the lads were put on the wire, many for as long as five hours. There were a lot of injuries, some serious – at least one man lost an eye – and there were loads of dog bites, rubber-bullet wounds, and badly bruised and broken limbs. They got it much worse than we did, but then, as T O'G said, "We fought with the head". I don't know if that's a fair comment, but maybe Your Man was right when he said the fire was the time to bob and weave – and leave.

Between swopping yarns which grew taller with each telling, we spent today scrounging through the rubble looking for souvenirs. Ted and I and wee Pat agreed to build a wee shelter. When Ted and I had it finished Pat deserted us for better accommodation. This evening we got a pint of milk plus two rounds of bread and margarine before retiring. There is no lock-up. There is nothing to lock up. We sleep where and when we want. There are scores of wee fires dotted around this cage, the same in all the others. Ted and I slept well despite the rain and wind. Our shelter is only two feet high, like a bivouac.

Friday October 18:
Spent the day watching the Commander rigging up a shower, out there in the open air among the much-diminished, blackened, twisted and gnarled aluminium walls of what used to be the toilets. He eventually got it going. Mr Sheen and

Bunjy were the first under it. The water was warm! We were promised stew but instead got two rounds of bread and margarine and a pint of milk. Big Dominic and Billy R organized a great sing-song around their fire.

Saturday October 19:
The stew came: British Army stew. It's little wonder they can't fight if that's what they call stew. They left out the Irish, and the mutton and the onions and the carrots and most of the spuds – but it was still delicious. We also got a big can of hot water for tea. The prison chaplains also arrived in with cigarettes. Real ones. They feel enormous between your lips after days of smoking wee Geordie's roll-ups. Gallagher's Blues abú. We got pea-soup this evening.

Sunday October 20:
Fr Joachim said mass. He's a monk. Fathers Toner and Cahill also called. They reckon the cold weather is keeping down disease. We're living in a shanty town. Stew again and bread and margarine, and cardboard boxes of clothes from all our friends outside. Up the Green Cross and An Cumann Cabhrach and Noraid and the Republican Welfare Committee. I had a shower. I never realized I was so dirty until I saw the streams of dirty water flowing from my beard. Also got some Condor Ready Rubbed for my pipe from one of the priests. We also each got an orange. Ah, such luxury. Life is great! Live for the moment: seize it! We had a fantastic concert tonight. We weren't going to go, but you know what? As we snuggled down together Big Ted turned to me and said, "I'm glad we went out tonight". So am I. But I hope the visits start soon. Ted's getting a bit bohemian.

Monday October 21:
Your Man started his tunnel. "At last," he said. Things are back to normal.

"Well, what do you think of that?" Cedric asked proudly.

"That's a bit of history you have there," Egbert replied.

"I know."

"It's a pity it doesn't include the solidarity actions by the women in Armagh, or the lads in the Crum who got beaten up, or the fire in Magilligan, but of course you wouldn't have known that," Egbert mused.

"It's a pity it's stinking," Your Man said. "The Public Records Office or the National Library Archives would never accept it in that condition. And, by the way, my role was more significant than you give me credit for."

"What!"

"I'm only joking! Ha, ha. You're too serious."

"And that's what wrong with you: you're never serious. You're a buck eejit."

"Y'reckon? And y'know why?"

"Why?"

"I only got serious twice in my life. The last time I took anything serious the judge couldn't see the funny side of it."

"What about the other time?"

"The other time I got serious I got married."

"Ach, piss off."

"Serious?"

"Nawh."

"Well, by the way, did I ever tell you about the escape from Newry courthouse? Listen . . ."

A FESTIVE BACK-STAB

"I see Cedric is knitting a scarf," Paddy Mo confided to his comrades in the half-hut.

"Ach well," said the Bellringer, "it will keep him quiet. He's never done complaining."

"I'm knitting a balaclava for whenever the snow comes. I'm always foundered when it's snowing," Cedric snorted.

"What are you making Alec?"

Alec is watching his budgies. He emerges a few seconds later with his finger on his lips.

"Sssshh," he whispers, "I think they're going to do it now."

The boys sneak over to Alec's locker. Egbert shepherds Paddy Mo and Ginty outside.

"Youse aren't allowed to watch," he commands. "You're too young."

While they protest, Sambo sneaks past, in between the two Blackies. McGlo is in the front row, of course. Alec enters proudly and pulls the slide back from his breeding box. The two budgies sit perched sleeping in the corner.

"They're not doing it at all," Bik snarls disappointedly.

"They won't do it while youse uns are all here," Alec whinges.

"Maybe after Christmas," Stewarty volunteers, "maybe they'll do it then."

"They've done it twice already," Alec protests. "Where's Thomas? Thomas . . ."

Thomas has fallen asleep (again) in the corner.

"Well I saw them doing it," Alec finishes lamely. "I saw . . ."

The boys drift away. Alec returns to his bunk. The budgies start doing it. Alec calls the boys back. Immediately the budgies go to sleep. Christmas is approaching the half-hut.

In the middle hut Bik listens intently to the BBC World Service on the radio. Honky Tonks keeps three separate conversations going at once and Skeet says his rosary quietly in the corner. The Dark and Soppy Walter, choked with Christmas spirit, are having an intimate talk about television programmes, long johns and the male menopause. The Doyle brothers, known to us all as the First and Second Doyles, write to their mammy and their daddies. The Five Sorrowful Mysteries weeps quietly in the toilet.

Crazy Joe, in the depths of a big D since Scobie left him, stares dejectedly at the blank TV screen and worries about his nose. The Hurdy Gurdy man polishes his boots, again. Cleaky polishes the top of his head, again. "Hair today, gone tomorrow," he mutters to himself.

Bloggs is engaged in lively conversation with Paul McNabb's budgies. Paul, confident that he will be a daddy before Alec's budgies even consider doing it, lies contentedly on his bunk.

Surely-to-God is finished making his nineteenth miniature piano and Pat Beag completes yet another plaque. At the hot-plate Noel Eile, Little John, Large Doc and Mickey D sing patriotic songs. Duicy John, Skin and Doris-Day-Clarke rehearse Christmas carols in Cheeser's locker. Moke and Dougie engage Swede, Bobby Breeze Block, Dickie Glen and Toby in a well-informed debate on the relative merits of *poitín* as against Drawbridge wine. Guts Donnelly writes to his wife. On the next bed, Twinkle Higgins writes to somebody else's wife. Paddy Mac hums "White Christmas" to himself.

Andy Goldfish is still writing to a namesake in America. A sad soulful letter. Joe B, as always cheerful, lies in a heap on his cross below Soppy Walter's bed. Wink-and-Nod decodes the card he received from his uncle, presently on CIA duty in Greece. Todler is eating, again. Jack the Giant loose-talks. Happy Horses blethers on. Che O'Hara writes to Downing Street demanding his release and a British withdrawal from Ireland.

It is Christmas week in the middle hut.

It is also Christmas week in the Gaeltacht hut. Burnsy continues with his life's work: he started reading *Liam Mellows* in 1974; he hopes to finish it any year now. Meanwhile, mourning the loss of his drink, he endeavours to play tin whistle, banjo, guitar and bodhrán all at the same time.

Danny D, wrecked since Dee's removal to Cage Thirteen (it's all Dosser's fault) lies alone, sad and deserted in Jack the Giant's pit, while Igor sits in a wee world of his own.

Heavy Head parcels up a packet of cigars for me (I hope) and Micko back-stabs his brother Joe. Mr Sheen threads his way, as always, through a piece of embroidery-work and Billy D parcels up another packet of cigars (I hope) for me. Big Sid rinses out his simmet in the sink.

Floorboards sits quietly on his bed, watching his budgies doing it. They haven't stopped doing it since he added *poitín* to their seed last week.

Doc, amazed at the way they're doing it, locks himself in his locker to admire his new hairstyle. T.C. sighs.

Johnser, in shorts, press-ups his way down the hut. Jaws talks on. Rigor Mortis sleeps through it all. Big Marshall smiles.

A huddle of countrymen gather in the toilet and discuss the price of mutton. Brendan Curran closes his shop for the night. Christmas settles in on us all.

In the study hut Dicky feeds his mouse. Sporty has arrived to deface Donal's drawings, and the Badger dissents.

And so Christmas slips past, the days made slippier by liberal doses of electric soup, or *poitín*, as some of the lesser-educated lads call it. I don't know how they can hide twenty gallons of the stuff in a cage this size and still have enough to get rightly stewed after even the most rigorous of raids. A touch of that stuff and a seasoning of Christmas cheer brings even the worst of bad enemies together. Old scores and older sores evaporate in bawdy choruses of "Jingle Bells".

"Oiche Chiúin" bursts from hoarse subversive throats. Backs, once stabbed, are anointed with hearty slaps and "Sound man ye are" is the order of the day. In the wee small hours misunderstandings are explained, explanations are accepted, hands are shaken, tears shed. Peace and goodwill reign supreme.

Even today, St Stephen's day, all are united in hangovers. A great, quiet, thumping, throbbing headache has taken over the entire camp and the silence is broken only by the muttering of the odd pale-faced stalwart who crawls painfully to *an leithreas*! Already rumours are starting to poke their credible little heads up:

"Did you hear about Harold down in Cage Ten? And Big Aodán down in Nine?"

"Big Bob was paraletic. He ..."

"You should have seen Alphonsus in our hut. He clocked out at five o'clock in the morning."

"Wait till you hear this. Thon fella who was away to be a priest was up until half-six. They had to put him to bed."

The *craic* was indeed fierce. A Derry wan, who compromised by singing the "Belfast Brigade" to the air of "Danny Boy", sits shaking and bleary-eyed to my left, while Egbert and Cedric plead for a bucket. Me? I'm wrecked.

Ooooops, the screws have just arrived for lock-up. A dipsomaniacal fatigue settles over Long Kesh as they secure us for the night.

I must go. I booked a seat for Floorboard's cell at ten

o'clock. I'm going to watch his budgies doing it. What's it Your Man says: *soixante-neuf*. Remember '69? Aye, nostalgia ain't what it used to be.

Ach, well. It's better than nothing at all.

SLÁINTE

"Did any of you see Cedric?" Egbert asked.

"He's with Dosser," a voice shouted back down the hut.

Egbert left with one of his smug little smiles on his face.

The Dosser was our brewmaster, our distiller. He and a motley crew of apprentices gathered up the ingredients, prepared them and stored them in containers which were then carefully hidden. While the rest of us waited, the Dosser performed intricate little rites, tests and other perambulations until, satisfied that his potions had matured, he commenced to erect his still. Then, as he explained it himself, he proceeded to "purify the brew by extracting its essence through heat vaporizing it, and then condensing it with cold and collecting the resulting liquid".

That's what he was doing the day Egbert was looking for Cedric. It didn't take Egbert long to find the Dosser; he tracked him down to his hidey-hole with a homing instinct an excise man would have envied.

"Is Cedric here?" he called.

"Nawh, he couldn't stand the pace. He left a while ago," Your Man, who was acting as assistant, replied good humouredly.

The Dosser said nothing. The making of *poitín* is an intricate process requiring great concentration and he was totally engrossed in his art. He was studying a list of figures, written neatly in a little black notebook. Dosser was a perfectionist.

"Did youse let him drink?" Egbert enquired.

"Couldn't stop him," Your Man smiled. "He had a note from his mammy."

"Very funny," Egbert snapped. "It's well seen youse don't have to live with him."

He went off in high dudgeon. The Dosser finished his calculations.

"I think we'll be okay," he turned to Your Man and Igor, "It's three o'clock now; this run will be finished and the other one started before five. That will get us finished by eight. We'll have everything stashed away before lock-up."

"An bhfuil Cedric anseo?" (Is Cedric here?) Egbert shouted into the Gaeltacht hut.

"Nawh, Ní fhaca mé é," (Nawh, I didn't see him) someone shouted back. "Nach bhfuil sé leatsa?" (Isn't he with you?)

"If he was with me I'd hardly be lookin' for him, would I?" Egbert snarled.

"Ná bí ag caint as Béarla," (Don't be talking English) the Gaeltacht Hut OC commanded.

"Go raibh bloody maith agat," (Thanks very bloody much). Egbert left.

The making of *poitín* requires a certain finesse and a degree of expertise. Especially in Long Kesh. Of the *poitín* makers I have known, the Dosser was probably the best organized, at least among the sentenced men. The internees had their own champions, and most of them swore by the Commander. Nevertheless, the honour of being the best makers of *poitín* would have to go to men from North Antrim, Tyrone, South Armagh or South Derry, some of whom can recall when every Irish village had its own distillery. That, they will tell you, was before

1661, when a tax was introduced. Nobody in South Derry, North Antrim, South Armagh or Tyrone paid it, nor would they drink the new "parliamentary whiskey". *Poitín* was their man. Here in Long Kesh their business is conducted on a small, selective scale – for gourmets. The Dosser and the Commander, like John Power and Arthur Guinness, cater for a wider clientele.

It is said that the Commander placed a monthly levy on all the occupants of his cage. Two pounds of sugar or six pounds of fruit were expected; with about 140 internees in his charge, that made for a goodly amount of raw material. The Commander came up with the yeast and he and his trusty men then laboured manfully to produce and consume gallons of alcohol with the regularity of a conveyer belt. Bushmills would have been threatened by such industry had the Commander taking up brewing as a legitimate concern. Dickie Glen, however, claimed that the Commander cut corners. In times of fruit shortage or blight potatoes were bribed from the camp kitchen to become an experimental and highly potent potato wine, which the Commander described as a cheeky little vintage.

The Commander held that you can make alcohol from nearly anything as long as you have sugar and yeast; the rest is just for taste, it's the alcohol which is important. He has an almost permanent slur in his speech and an increasingly punch-drunk, John Wayne walk. The Dosser took a different view: for him the taste was almost as important as alcohol content. Apples and oranges were his preferred and most constant base though, in rare circumstances, he had been known to use jail jam. He nearly always had some kind of concoction fermenting away somewhere. Most Long Kesh distillers, like the Commander, calculated when the next raid was likely. They hurriedly squashed together their ingredients, fermented them for about eight days, ran them through a worm and got drunk. But the Dosser was different: his hiding places or dumps were carefully constructed and some of his brew survived for six months, simmering gently in the innards of our cage until the potent smell demanded that it be moved on to the next part of the process. The Dosser left nothing to chance. All his deposits were graded according to age, content, quantity and temperature of the dump. All relevant information was recorded – in code, of course.

During the first part of the fermentation process the Dosser checked and rechecked his cellars, notebook and pen in hand and the ever faithful Igor, his number one apprentice, by his side. When the Dosser was satisfied that everything had reached its optimum maturity he assembled his still and the distilling commenced. Then and only then were the chosen and carefully selected batches brought forward.

The first run was the most potent and normally it had to be diluted. If it was a big run or if he was feeling particularly generous, Dosser presented a sample to his helpers. Cedric had received such a sample the day he went into hiding from Egbert. At least, Egbert says he went into hiding: Cedric says he never went anywhere, he just became invisible. In fact he fell into a drunken slumber behind the shower hut and it took almost two hours for Egbert's searching, sober eyes to locate him. When Cedric would wake an hour later, he would be a changed person.

Meanwhile, Dosser had assembled forty-two pints of clear-spirited moonshine. He also supplied a sort of scrumpy – nine gallons in this batch – for those who liked a pint with their wee ones. It was approaching eight o'clock when the last of the *poitín* was drained from the wash. Dosser was well satisfied.

"Let's get cleared up men," he suggested. "A wee walk before lock-up would be just the ticket before we get down to some serious drinking."

Back in the hut Big Duice thought he should try to console Egbert about Cedric's unprecedented absence.

"Maybe Cedric got a transfer to another cage," he suggested delicately.

Egbert never even bothered to answer him but just smiled his crooked little smile.

Cedric was lying in the yard, his face painted bright green, with two yellow strokes where his eyebrows had used to be. His eyebrows and half of his moustache had been shaved off. Egbert had done his work well: having used only the best leather dyes, it would be three weeks before Cedric's visage would return to its normal rosy pallor. But Cedric was oblivious to all this. He was stocious; he felt great. He managed to get a finger-hold in the tarmac and inched his way towards the wire. He sang Leonard Cohen ditties tunefully to the ground. He elbowed himself slowly over on his back. "Songs for a suicide," he chided the stars. "Let's sing something more in keeping with our mood. Moonlight and roses bring wonderful memories of you," he crooned.

It was fifteen minutes to lock-up. Dosser's still was now once again part of the plumbing in the shower hut. His customers had received their supplies – all except Cedric and Egbert; Your Man brought their bevy to Egbert's bunk.

"Here you are, old friend," he told Egbert, "that's free, gratis and for nothing for you and your mucker."

"He's still not in," Egbert replied. "I hope he hasn't got himself into trouble." He barely smothered a grin.

Cedric had reached the cage wire. A British soldier, complete with a large alsatian dog, faced him on the other side of the wire.

"Alsatians once again, alsatians once again," Cedric sang to them both, to the air of "A Nation Once Again".

"I see you're taking your mother for a walk," he said pleasantly to the Brit.

"F_____ off! Away from that wire, you Paddy lunatic f _____ r," the Brit snarled, unnerved at the green-faced apparition which crouched before him.

"G'wan back to your own country, you foul-mouthed English glyp," Cedric retorted.

He pulled himself up slowly, fingers clutching the wire

until he was in a vertical position. The Brit faced him uneasily. The war-dog growled manacingly. Then, finally erect, Cedric addressed them. His strong, proud Ulster voice boomed across the wire and even the dog was silenced as Cedric proclaimed:

"We are the indomitable Irishry. You are mere tools of the colonisers. You cannot defeat us. You do not understand us. Time has triumphed," he orated, "the wind has scattered all. Empires are lost. Even England will bite the dust. Or in other words," he continued,

"Ireland was Ireland, when England was a pup,
Ireland will be Ireland, when England's buggered up."

The Brit drew his baton and struck the wire at Cedric's face while the dog lunged forward snarling and snapping.

"Ach, catch yourself on," Cedric chortled. "You can stick your wooden baton up your hole," he chanted.

"You can stick your wooden baton up your hole.
You can shove your wooden baton, shove your wooden baton,
You can shove your wooden baton up your hole," he laughed.

The Brit kicked the wire and smashed at it with his baton. Cedric stood back.

"A wee bit of order," he cried. "Bígí ciúin. One singer, one song. A wee bit of order for the singer. I'll start youse off with this wee one, and then youse can join in the chorus. OK?

"Show me the man who does not love the land where he was born,
Who does not look on it with pride no matter how forlorn.
I only know that I love mine and I hope one day to see
Oppression driven from our shores and Ireland one day free.
"This is the chorus," he intoned. "Join in if you like.
"Let friends all turn against me, let folks say what they will,
My heart is in my country and I love old Ireland still.

"Arís – all together now. Let friends all turn . . ."

The Dosser burst into the hut. "There's trouble at the wire!" he exclaimed. "It's that stumer Cedric! He's winding up a Brit. If we don't get him away before the screws arrive in for lock-up he's going to get our drink caught," he informed Egbert.

"That's all you're worried about, isn't it? No thought for anyone else. No thought for poor Cedric. If the OC sees him he'll be on punishment for a year," Egbert lamented as he leapt from his bunk.

At the wire Cedric had Egbert in his thoughts. "OK," he challenged the soldier. "The next raid just ask for Egbert. That's me. That's my hut," he gestured and then, seeing Egbert speeding towards him across the yard, "Just ask for me," he concluded, "'cos I want to knock your bollocks in. You and me: a fair dig. Up the Murph!"

"Whoa," Egbert cut in. "Hold your horses comrade," he told Cedric. "Can you not leave him alone," he chided the enraged Brit. "Pick on someone your own size next time, OK?

"C'mon mucker," he led Cedric away from the wire. "Do you fancy a wee drink? Who did that to your face?" he queried. "Let's go in now before lock-up. We don't want any trouble, do we?"

They laughed together, each delighting in his own mischief-making, unaware of the other's.

"Trouble? Trouble?" Cedric stopped and braced himself. "You don't know the half of it, Egbert," he chuckled, his green visage wrinkling in a smile.

"I know you don't," Egbert agreed.

"Trouble?" Cedric queried. "I'll give them trouble.

"If you hate the British army, clap your hands," he sang.

"If you hate the British army, clap your hands.

If you love the IRA, if you love the IRA,

If you hate the Lazy K, clap your hands."

Egbert opened the door of the hut and dunted Cedric, still singing, inside. Your Man handed them both a drink.

"The night is young," he announced with a flourish towards the waiting pints of pure. "I like your make-up," he told Cedric, who stared back at him, green and uncomprehending.

"Let's have a toast," Egbert suggested.

They raised their jam jars in salute to each other.

"Sláinte," said Your Man to Cedric.

"Up the RA," Cedric declared, his green face beaming at us all.

"Up the RA!" we all replied in unison.

Then, raising our drinks to him and to Egbert and to Your Man in a happy chorus, we grinned and toasted one and other.

"Sláinte!" we proclaimed.

TERRORISM

I was just blimping through my copy of the Northern Ireland (Emergency Provisions) Act 1973, and Part (IV) Miscellaneous and General gives a definition of terrorism.

> Terrorism means the use of violence for political ends and includes any use of violence for the purpose of putting the public or any section of the public in fear.

Now, dear readers, how does that grab you? It's wonderful what you can do with words, isn't it?

I was thinking to myself, being in jail and all that, of all the people I know who are involved in terrorism. No, I don't mean you and me! I mean all the people who fit into the above definition. It would take a few volumes to go over all the categories which immediately flip through my little mind so, to be parochial about it, I will deal with one category only. It is a special category all on its own. Would you believe I mean the people in charge of prisoners, here and in England? I'll tell you what I'll do. I'll just slide over a few of their recent activities and you can work out for yourself whether they can be described as above. Sound?

The first thing I want you all to do is to consider reports of the Balcome Street trial. The *craic* is this: the men involved have claimed responsibility for the Guildford and Woolwich bombings. To date they have supplied a solicitor with separate statements of how they carried out these operations and, from what I read, the statements are so detailed and precise that there can be no doubting their authenticity. Furthermore, witnesses are available to swear that there was no collusion between the men when they wrote the statements and that each statement was given voluntarily.

The only difficulty is that the British state has already jailed other people for causing these explosions. Other people who have consistently claimed that they were framed, that they were forced to sign confessions, and that they are innocent. Other people who were arrested simply because the British couldn't catch the IRA units involved. So they invented "IRA units" they could catch.

One obvious point which arises is why and how do innocent people come to sign statements, and how do those who don't sign still manage to end up doing long sentences? Surely the British police, the judiciary and the prison systems aren't guilty of "the use of violence for political ends" or of "putting a section of the public in fear"?

And what of the beatings handed out in Albany recently? I wonder how Sean Campbell received a broken arm, jaw and leg, plus fractured ribs? How did Father Fell come by a broken nose? How did others receive severe bruising and head injuries? Maybe they all fell down stairs together?

Which brings me to the case of Eddie Byrne. Last week Eddie suffered a dislocated shoulder while in Parkhurst Prison on the Isle of Wight. And what of Patrick Hackett, who is now in solitary in Brixton Prison? Patrick, who had lost a hand and a leg in an explosion, was given solitary for not walking around an exercise yard.

There are many other cases of Irish prisoners receiving mysterious injuries and long stretches in solitary. A Scottish solicitor, Alastair Logan, has published in the *Law Guardian*, the journal of the London Law Society, a well-researched and documented indictment of the treatment of Republican prisoners held in British prisons. He also includes descriptions of injuries received by Irish people while in police custody or on remand.

An *Irish Press* editorial of 20 December 1976 comments:

> The descriptions in Mr Logan's article of the harassment to which Republican prisoners are subjected, make painful reading. The restrictions on visits by relatives, clergymen and lawyers, the humiliating strip-searches, the limited access to reading material . . . the denial of education and recreational facilities are chronicled in a depressing sequence. What must it be like to spend all one's time in a cell where the light is on 24 hours a day?

So much, dear readers, of England. What then of Ireland?

Solitary confinement was condemned as far back as the end of the nineteenth century by a British Parliamentary Committee. Today in Long Kesh Republican prisoners are held in solitary twenty-four hours a day. They are naked, have no contact with the outside world (newspapers, letters, visits etc. are stopped), no exercise facilities, and they can expect to continue in this manner for the foreseeable future.

Solitary confinement is an unpleasant, soul-destroying and mind-bending experience. Imagine yourself locked in a coal-shed for a week, naked, with no means of communicating with the world outside. Imagine the up-roar in our newspaper columns and halls of learning if this activity was uncovered in South Africa, Chile or Rhodesia. Yet it is happening now, and only a few hundred yards from where I write.

The Association for Legal Justice has condemned what it calls the lack of humanity shown by the British government's Northern Ireland Office in its treatment of these prisoners. "Just as serious," their statement continues, "is the rising tide of worry and resentment being generated among their families and relations . . ."

I wonder if this practice fits into the British definition of "putting the public or any section of the public in fear"?

Fr Faul, in an address to a recent conference on prisoners' rights, declared: "I have a big doubt in my mind about the regime in Portlaoise Prison . . . it is disimproving the men and producing hardened and embittered persons."

The Dublin government minister responsible for Portlaoise, in a BBC interview during the recent controversy surrounding the declaration of a State of Emergency, declared: "We intend to finish this thing once and for all". He didn't say that his government wouldn't use violence, and it is common knowledge that prisoners in Free State jails are ill-treated and confined to solitary. One prisoner, Tom Smith, was shot dead while "attempting to escape". It is also common knowledge that severe restrictions on visits by relatives, lawyers and clergymen have been imposed in Portlaoise and Limerick jails. Two bishops have been refused permission to visit prisoners, as have the parish priests of some of the men.

Despite evidence of beatings, despite the deaths of prisoners, despite the verdict at Strasbourg, despite commissions, tribunals and inquiries, no British soldier, RUC man, policeman or screw has ever served a day in prison since 1969 for murder or torture committed while on duty.

The reason for this is that British laws, like the one which defines terrorism, have neat Catch 22 clauses built in. The Northern Ireland (Emergency Provisions) Act, for example, "applies to persons who have attained the age of fourteen and are not serving members of Her Majesty's regular naval, military or air force". Yahoo!

Would the real terrorists stand up, please?

SUCH A YARN

In olden times in Ireland, *i bhfad, bhfad ó shoin*, there was a great man of the Clann de Béal. He was called Malachi, alias the Heathen. He had a great castle or rath at Dún Dealgan (Dundalk) and whenever the English government was striving to put some wrong on the country, he was always the man who stood against it.

He was a really cracking fighter, a first-class leader and very skilful with any class of weapon. And, as well as all this, he could change himself into any shape he wanted. Now, his wife knew that he had this power and she was always nagging at him to let her into his secret but, being a wise man and a bit of a chauvinist to boot, he wouldn't have any of it. Well, at least not in the beginning.

She nagged and nagged and nagged, however, until poor old Malachi was worn and wrecked. He tried putting her off, he messed her around but, eventually, he was obliged to give in. He agreed to turn himself into a blackbird right before her eyes. There was only one catch: if she showed the slightest hint of fear he would be finished, and would not recover his natural form for ages and ages and ages. Of course, the wife promised that she wouldn't be frightened and that, indeed, he would be proud of her.

So, one beautiful summer evening, as they were sitting

in their grand drawing-room, he turned his face away from her, muttered some words and, before you could shout "Yahoo!" he had disappeared and a lovely blackbird was flying about the room.

The wife, for all her boasting, was a wee bit scared, but she held her own pretty well, especially when he came and perched on her shoulder and fluttered his wings at her, and put his little beak to her lips and whistled the delightfullest tune you ever did hear. He flew in circles around the room and played Ralioh with her, and flew out into the garden and back again, and lay down on her lap as if asleep before jumping up once more.

Now this went on for a good while and when the two of them were finished carrying on he took one more flight into the open air. It was only a second before he was back but the next minute a great big hawk was in through the window after him! The wife gave one loud scream, though there was no need for the wild bird shot into the room and crashed into the table with such force that it was killed, stone dead, on the spot.

The wife's promise had been broken. She had shown her fear and so, when she looked around for the blackbird, it was nowhere to be seen. It had disappeared, and she was never to lay eyes on Malachi again.

That's not the end of the story, not by a long straw. You see, Malachi and his warriors are now sleeping in a long cavern under the rath at Dundalk. There is a table running through the middle of the cave. Malachi is sitting at its head and his troopers, complete in armour, are ranged along either side, their heads resting in their arms. Their horses, saddled and bridled, stand behind them. And when the day comes for the miller's son, who will be born with six fingers on each hand, to blow his trumpet, the horses will stomp and whinny and the knights awaken and mount their steeds and go forth into battle to chase the English government and troops out of Ireland.

And that day, dear comrades, has yet to arrive. But in

the meantime, every seven years Malachi rides round the Curragh of Kildare on a great grey donkey whose silver shoes were half an inch thick at the time of Malachi's disappearance. When these shoes are worn down as thin as a cat's ear, and even if the miller's son does not sound the trumpet, Malachi will be restored to the society of living men and women. He will fight a great battle with the English and reign as King of Ireland for two score years after he drives them out of the country.

On the nights that he rides around the Curragh the entrance to the cavern at Dundalk may be seen by anyone chancing to pass by. About a hundred years ago over a dozen people saw it, and only last month a man actually found his way into it as he returned home from the Fianna Fail *Árd Fheis*. He was a horse-dealer by vocation and a Fianna Fail minister by trade. It was late when he saw the lighted cavern and he nipped inside for a second. He had a few drinks taken but the lights and the stillness and the sight of the men in armour soon sobered him up.

His hands began to tremble and he let a bridle fall on the ground. The sound echoed and re-echoed through the long cave and one of the warriors just next to him lifted his head and said, in a deep hoarse voice, "Is it time yet?"

The horse-dealer trembled and replied, "No, not yet – but it won't be long now," and the warrior sank down once more.

So there you are.

Having told you all this I wonder if the next time you're in Dundalk you would have a look for that cavern? And if you find it, sneak in through the door and look at Malachi, his warriors and their horses, sleeping, just waiting for the day when they will ride out. Make sure there are no Fianna Fail ministers in the vicinity. Then stand well back, and scream at the top of your voice: "C'mon, wake up! Now's the time!"

Until then, mother Ireland, please: get off my back!

BEWARE THE IDES OF MARCH

Jail is a different place without visits. For one thing, everyone soon stops washing themselves. Cedric, as always full of initiative, had stopped earlier than anyone else. He was a dirty, leaping, pigging and unshaven mess. Except for his head. He had his head shaved. For some reason many POWs shave their heads during visit stoppages. Seamus Beag MacDairire O'Goboney, our learned Celtic scholar and creative marxist-in-residence, traces this practice back to an ancient Irish pagan ritual. Something to do with fertility rites.

We were all crowded around Cedric's bunk playing cards and wirelessing – that is, talking away – as best we could. But Cedric was shooting off his mouth and nobody else could get a word in with his monopoly on the conversation.

Then he stopped. We all looked up in surprise. It's hard to explain to anyone who doesn't know him, but you can take it from me that it is most unusual for Cedric to stop talking. Especially like that. And he did seem to be having genuine difficulty.

His face was turning a deep purple, even deeper than it usually is, and the eyes were bulging goldfishingly. Only a weak croak escaped from between his lips, yet they kept moving, forming words but remaining wordless. His face became contorted and sweat broke on his brow.

We all stared silently at him, afraid to interfere and seemingly powerless to intervene. There was something happening among us, something untouchable, indescribable, but there still the same; something definite yet indefinable. Something was happening to us and to Cedric and he was combating that something. We all knew this as if by instinct. We knew that a struggle between good and evil, a struggle for control, was being fought before our eyes. And then it stopped. Just as suddenly as it had begun, it ceased.

Cedric's face cleared, a deep whistle escaped his lips, he gave a shake – almost dog-like – cleared his throat, grinned sheepishly and exclaimed: "What were we talking about?"

"You mean, what were you talking about," I replied cruelly.

Egbert stopped us getting any further involved for, at that minute, he trumped his partner (for the umpteenth time that night) and our card game was over.

It was only when I was drifting off to sleep an hour or so later that I thought back to our card game. As my mind slipped from the realities of Long Kesh into my own personal dreamworld, Cedric's face pushed past thoughts of my wife and family and his question bounced into my sleep: "What *were* we talking about?"

And it's only now that I understand what happened: it came to me during the news this evening. I had known that something was missing, that something had changed, but I hadn't been able to put my finger on what it was. But it's all so clear now that I'm writing about it and I honestly don't know why it didn't dawn on me before. I remember that Cedric lost track of his revolutionary discourse at exactly twelve o'clock last night. Up till then we had been discussing the Stormont Convention, or the lack of it, but as midnight brought us into the first day of

March Cedric was cut off in mid-sentence. It didn't affect us all as dramatically as that, but then we weren't talking as much. Nevertheless, British direct ruler Merlyn Rees's new act came into being at twelve midnight and suddenly we stopped being political prisoners. That's as clear as day. As soon as the legislation came into effect, Irishmen and women in the goals all over the North became criminals. It was like an act of God.

I can see Cedric's face now as I'm writing. I can recall the change which came over all of us. Why the hell didn't I catch on before this?

Today we had all sensed that something was wrong, something was different. The way I felt compelled to hand over my books to the screws. The way we *all* formed a queue at the gate and surrendered our books to the screws: books on Irish history, on republicanism, on revolutionary theory. I didn't know why I did it, but it seemed to be the right thing to do. Sean O'Casey, *Buntús Cainte*; Fintan Lalor, *Fios Feasa*: all our prized literature found its way to the wee bonfire just outside the cage.

The change was so obvious I don't know how I could have missed it. I should have known as soon as I addressed the screws as "sir".

"Please sir," I had snivelled, "could I have a paint-brush and some paint?"

"They are in the cage already," he had replied, pointing to where Nigel was covering our wall-painting of the 1916 Proclamation with black prison paint.

And the way the whole fibre of our command structure here had suddenly slumped. I should have known when the lectures, debates and discussions were cancelled earlier today. Hell's Gates – we should all have twigged when the screws took us for drill!

It's easy to talk now, of course, but when you think of it, I suppose it's not as easy as all that. After all, there is something supernatural in the way Brit laws govern us. What else could we have done when faced with laws passed by the Westminster House of Commons? It's OK scoffing at it now, but you should have seen the fight Cedric put up. And, as I've said, I didn't catch on until after the late news. I'm probably the only one here who does know, too, because I'm the only one here who watched it. All the boys watched the late movie but cleared off when it was over. I was doing the same thing myself when I spilled my tea and as I stopped to mop the floor, I alone heard the announcer announce: "Political status for special category prisoners has ceased in Northern Ireland. All prisoners are now criminals. This affects 1,500 prisoners, of which 900 were Republicans."

And then I remembered!

It took time. It came to me slowly as I recalled why I'm here. Why Long Kesh is here; why the Brits are here.

I tried to explain it to Your Man as we did a few laps of the yard tonight before lock-up. I didn't seem to get through though. He just grinned at me and chortled idiotically, "Come again?"

"We're ordinary criminals now," I informed him.

"So we're all OCs after all," he joked.

I left him at that; I was getting nowhere. Not that I blame him – everybody knows the effect a Brit law can have on a person. As soon as it becomes the law of the land, *sin é*. It's worked for years now. You've only to look at how the Dublin establishment behaves or at sections of the media. But still, it's hard to legislate for everything.

Yesterday's *Daily Mirror* for example. I read it from cover to cover. I seem compelled to read papers like that now. And on page five it had a letter which asked: "Why do we call the Icelandic boats 'gunboats' and our own boats 'frigates'? Our boats are bigger than the Icelandic boats and have more guns on them. Do we have to make the Icelanders appear more aggressive? Are we biased?"

That letter writer is like me. For some reason the laws don't affect him, at least not completely. He knows that there is something wrong, even if he's not sure what it is. But it's hard to see it clearly.

Merlyn Rees, though: he has the advantage. Merlyn

knows he has the power to change people's motivation, people's reasoning, people's attitudes. All he has to do is get a law passed and we are all compelled to obey it. It's as simple as that.

After all, you can't support criminals, and there is nothing we poor Irish can do if the mighty British government passes legislation to prove it. Haven't Merlyn Rees, Harold Wilson, Gerry Fitt, Thomas Passmore, Cardinal Conway, William Cosgrave, Conor Cruise, Ian Paisley, Uncle Tom Cobbley and all told us so?

I must go now. God bless England. Is there a world out there?

THE ÁRD FHEIS

The Cage OC, an amiable enough chap beneath his godfatherly facade, realized towards the end of his summing up that the body of the hall might have felt he was being over critical, and as his dormant but easily aroused inferiority complex assumed control he mumbled our historic first, but highly successful *Árd Fheis* to a close.

Delegates from Belfast, Strabane, Dungannon, Newry and Ballymurphy had travelled from the half-hut, the middle hut and the Gaeltacht for the two-day annual Sinn Fein *Árd Fheis* in the canteen. A veteran observer remarked that it was the biggest crowd he had ever seen at a non-compulsory meeting in Long Kesh during his five years of in-depth observations here. Militant left-wingers from the middle hut conversed amiably with the headcases from the half-hut, and awkward country lads studied proposals with an alertness which belied their accents. Business opened slowly but with the ratification of standing orders and the selection of a chairperson (who talked his way into the job) our own wee captive *Árd Fheis* commenced to wade its way through a long list of proposals.

First to speak was Brendan Hughes who proposed that Sinn Fein organize a massive agitation campaign in the Free State and that they affiliate themselves with all anti-state groups. He spoke of the need to exploit the mistakes being made by the Cosgrave government and detailed the recent history of collaboration and sell-out, of the blatant pro-British attitudes of Conor Cruise O'Brien, Cosgrave and Garret FitzGerald. Dee Delaney seconded the motion and brought delegates to their feet with his impassioned attack on the social, economic and political policies being implemented by the constitutional parties in Leinster House.

"Sinn Fein needs to ally itself with the people in their class struggle; we must instigate agitation not to reform the system but to change it," he declared. "Our agitation should be revolutionary agitation directed against the state and its lackeys."

The chairperson had difficulty containing delegates who stamped their feet and yelled support for Dee and the whole hall erupted in wild applause as Brendan Hughes in his summing up called upon Republicans to declare their own State of Emergency.

Needless to say the proposal was passed unanimously. A brief but rather nasty discussion then took place between Soppy Walter, a small pressure group which wanted procedural changes and the chairperson. At this point democracy was infringed upon, but quickly restored with the appearance of the above-mentioned Cage OC and the Cage Adjutant at the platform table. Seating themselves on either side of the chairperson they appeared to be taking notes. Soppy Walter went quiet.

Gerry Rooney, proposing the encouragement by Sinn Fein of anti-imperialist unity among working-class groups, was seconded by Tom Boy. Both speakers emphasized the way in which imperialists maintained unity and asked should not anti-imperialists learn a lesson from this? It was a commonsense move for us to make. A lot of delegates spoke on this issue. The Sticks got a bit of a bashing and finally, on the acceptance of an amendment – that Sinn Fein identify with *all* true anti-imperialist groups throughout the world – the motion was carried.

Next item on the *clár*. Wee Denis and Scobie proposed the updating of the Eire Nua booklet while Joe Floorboards and Surely-to-God called for the implementation of an education programme in all *cumann* areas. Denis in his proposal dealt at length with the need for an updating of Sinn Fein pamphlets, particularly policy documents, and of the need for members to be fully aware and conversant with policy. Scobie, in seconding this proposal, said that he had nothing to say. A heated discussion followed with Moke putting a strong case for the proposal. Soppy Walter proposed that the motion be put, which it eventually was, and it was carried then with two votes against and one abstention from Soppy Walter.

Joe Floorboards' and Surely-to-God's proposal followed the same pattern. Joe spoke of the great need for education. The basis, he declared, was at hand; ordinary people should be involved in get-togethers with Republicans, and we should explain our attitudes, our tactics, our policy. People should be able to complain and criticize; they should be part of it all and fully aware of what was happening. Education for Republicans, both in and outside the movement, was the beginning, the kernel, the foundation for everything. The motion was carried. Sambo for some reason abstained and Heithy didn't bother voting. Soppy Walter intervened on seven points of order.

Burnsie and Wee Paddy then proposed the immediate establishment of People's Councils in all areas. Burnsie, famous for his footballing abilities, emphasized the importance of People's Councils as a necessary part of the struggle. Nobody could understand what Paddy was talking about but in the discussion which followed Moke, Sambo and Soppy Walter all supported the motion. Noel McNabb also spoke and the proposal calling for the establishment of People's Councils was carried with only one vote in opposition.

Sunday's business concluded when the *Árd Fheis* went into private session for discussions on propaganda and publicity, but an informed source close to the Cage Staff informed me that Martin and Danny D steered their proposal through a rather stormy session, that Soppy Walter was joined by Padre Pio in heckling and that the chairperson had difficulty in maintaining order. I was also informed that Paddy Mac and Larry O' were able to squeeze their proposal to a victorious vote despite stiff opposition. The chairperson, bringing the private session to a close, told delegates that they would reconvene on Monday at two o'clock. The delegates then adjourned to their respective cells.

On Monday business began with a proposal from Dan D, Ripley McBangers and MacLiam Wilson calling for the distribution of republican literature, papers and policy documents throughout all areas regardless of the loss of capital involved. A subdued but intense discussion followed and the proposal was finally carried with only one abstention. Hugh Up and Bik McFarlane then pushed a proposal for a Sinn Fein campaign in favour of the teaching of Irish history and the Irish language in local schools, and for the promotion of Irish traditonal music in local social clubs. Padre Pio proposed an amendment which took a little of the sting out of that part of the proposal which dealt with the promotion of traditional music in clubs. The original proposal called for all musicians and singers to be paid a reasonable fee plus free drinks. The amendment limited the free drinks to one and referred the matter of fees to the clubs' committees.

The next three proposals were dealt with again in private session and cage officials were very tight-lipped about their outcome. One prominent dissident told me that the proposals were of a strictly internal nature but even he refused to disclose details about them. I gather that Rigor Mortis, Stu Mor, Malachy Deas, the Cat, Cleaky Clarke and Wee Dickie all proposed or seconded motions regarding political status, the Sinn Fein *Árd Chomhairle*, and other such matters. None of these gentlemen was available for comment but a spokesman for

Rigor said it was usual practice for delegates to remain silent on internal matters.

The last proposal, from Brendan Curran and Tommy Carroll, was passed unanimously. They called for the sending of an *Árd Fheis* report to all jails. The chairperson proposed a vote of thanks to himself, and the *Árd Fheis* concluded with a lengthy but well-delivered summing up by the Cage OC. Delegates were asked to forward proposals to Tom Hartley or to their local Sinn Fein *cumann*. At this point Soppy Walter and Padre Pio withdrew. Padre wanted the proposals to go to Danny Morrisson and Soppy Walter argued that they should cut out all middle-men and deal directly with Dublin. After withdrawing they reconvened for a back-stabbing session in Padre Pio's cell before returning to the *Árd Fheis*. It is believed that the majority of responsible delegates continued, as always, to ignore them.

In an exclusive interview the Cage OC and Adjutant told me that they considered the *Árd Fheis* to have been a great success, and hoped Sinn Fein *cumainn* outside would give a favourable reception to proposals sent out to them. The interest that POWs maintained in events outside was amply illustrated by the high level of debate and by the informed arguments put forward. Proposals on education, propaganda and People's Councils showed that Republican prisoners were well aware of the issues facing the struggle. They would await with interest a report from the *Árd Fheis* outside and promised, somewhat pessimistically, that the cage would probably have an *Árd Fheis* again next year.

The chairperson, incidentally, was Cleaky Clarke (senior). Himself, Soppy Walter and Padre Pio are still arguing away somewhere. In keeping with republican tradition they had walked out before the end of the session on a point of principle. Nobody can recall exactly what it was.

Egbert, Cedric and Your Man did not attend our *Árd Fheis* as a result of disagreements between themselves and the chairperson over seating arrangements. It is reported that they and the Doyle brothers met in the drying hut. *Scéal* has it that Your Man says our *Árd Fheis* was illegal and that theirs is the official Cage *Árd Fheis*. He says that the presence of the First and Second Doyles at their session gives it a historical legitimacy and makes ours an illegal assembly.

I wonder who he thinks he is? Or who he's trying to wind up? Some people never know when they're going too far.

H-BLOCK

"C'mon and we'll have a yarn with the two new lads," Cedric suggested. "They were kept overnight in the H-Block so we might get some *scéal* about Kieran Nugent."

"When were they sentenced?"

"On Wednesday," said Egbert, "and they got it pretty rough. Twenty years and sixteen years. The judges are making up for the fifty percent remission. It's all a cod. The Brits make great publicity about fifty percent remission and then quietly increase the sentences."

"How did the new lads get into the H-Block?"

"Ach, the screws were just messing about. C'mon and we'll get a few laps and we'll find out what the score is. *Ceart*?"

So away we went, me, Cedric and Egbert. We picked up the new lads on the way out of the hut and together the five of us made our way round the yard. The camp was almost deserted and, with the frost warning us of the winter ahead, we walked briskly. Cedric broke the silence first. He finds it hard to remain quiet for long.

"How did youse get brought into the H-Block?" he asked the younger of our two companions.

"They just brought us up from court and wheeled us round."

"Were the screws nasty?"

"Well, when we were brought there we were checked out by the head buck-cat, the SO. He was very cocky."

"He's always cocky," Cedric sniggered. "The poor man doesn't know what ails him."

"Like, the other screw wasn't too bad," our new man volunteered, "he just let us know that they were the bosses but he didn't give us any of the usual."

"He told me not to be writing on the walls, no singing and no ringing the bell unless I was dying," our other child interrupted.

"Well, they gave me a piss-pot and showed me how the lights worked," his comrade added.

"Very kind," Cedric said, "did they strip youse?"

"They stripped me," said our first man, "they thought I was staying . . ."

"And they bantered me for shouting over to Kieran Nugent," our second youngster butted in. "It was after they gave us the grub. It was bogging, oul' cold spuds, and I was up at the window trying to shout to Kieran. They keep him on his own. I was just yelling to let him know that there was some of us about the place and the screw came to the window, pretty nasty like, and told me there was no talking after lock-up, and if I was caught at the window again he would put me in a cell where no one would hear me. He was an ignorant sort of chap. Kieran Nugent didn't hear me anyway, or at least he didn't answer me. And I didn't want to push my luck with the screws."

"Ah, I know the type," grunted Cedric. "How long were you there?"

"Only until half-seven the next morning. They must have known I was coming up here, 'cos they took me out to the boards. Only one screw. He did a bit of wisecracking. He gave me a bible and took my shoes off me." He nodded to his comrade, "That's when I saw you. You had only a blanket on."

"Aye," said our martyred companion, "they wouldn't let us talk to each other."

"After that I was locked in the cell for a few hours," our second man ended.

"You got off light," said Cedric, "but how did you go?"

We all turned to the lad who had been stripped.

"Well, I was told I was coming up here and then about half an hour later another screw came in and asked me if I had any charges after the first of March. I told him that I had an IRA membership charge running from July 2nd to March 15th, and he told me I had lost my status."

"A kind of calendar justice," quipped Cedric. "Thank God I got caught before we became criminals. I only missed being a criminal by a few months, you know."

"Well, after I was told I'd lost my status, the first screw went away and returned with another screw. They were carrying a monkey suit. One of them told me to put it on. I told him there was no way I would wear it. We had a bit of a nark then 'cos he told me to call him sir, and he yelled a bit about not liking my attitude. Of course, I wouldn't call him sir ..."

"Hard-liner," Cedric grinned.

"... and the other screw grabbed me by the neck. He told me then that I could put the suit on and do eight years, get a visit once a week, and put on my own clothes at night. Or I could strip, wear a blanket, get no visits and do sixteen years. I asked to see the Governor and they told me I could put a request in in the morning for a governor, a priest or a doctor if I was a good boy."

"Helpful chaps," Cedric suggested.

"Then they made me strip. When I was finished they gave me a blanket and they left, taking my clothes with them. About half an hour later I was put into another cell. They took the mattresses and the bedclothes out. The cell was very cold. I was only getting warmed up, you know, by walking up and down, when they moved me again."

"A kind of republican movement," said Cedric.

"A short while after that another screw came and asked me where my clothes were. I think they had just realized that they had made a mistake. I told him that I didn't know and away he went. A little later they threw me in my gear and shortly after I was taken up here."

"So you were a political prisoner, then a criminal, then a political prisoner again," Cedric mused. "Funny how they work it all out."

"Oh, on Thursday night I saw one of the six that were caught at the Ritz. He told me that the screws were beating them about. And about sixteen remands arrived from the Crum just as I was leaving."

"Did any of youse see Kieran Nugent?" I asked.

"No, I never heard a word about him," said our first man.

"And what about you?" asked Cedric, "did you see or hear anything of young Nugent?"

"No," said our second man, "they keep him on his own. I don't think anyone sees him. It's a big place, you know. A fellow could be there and you'd never know what was happening to him."

THE TWELFTH

We were seated in our usual spot beside the shower hut. Cedric had successfully killed another conversation: all afternoon he had been spewing forth useless pieces of information, contradicting and taking issue with everything everyone said. When he gets contrary like that we usually keep quiet and wait for him to go away. He refused to leave, so we sat together in silence.

Outside on the Blairis Cemetery Road an Orangeman was beating his brains out on a Lambeg drum. Egbert was moved to break up our dummies' meeting.

"Did youse ever hear Seamus Heaney's poem about Orange drums?" Faced with the eloquence of our silence he cleared his throat. "Listen to this.

"The Lambeg balloons at his belly, weighs
Him back on his haunches, lodging thunder
Grossly there between his chin and his knees.
He is raised up by what he buckles under.

Each arm extended by a seasoned rod,
He parades behind it. And though the drummers
Are granted passage through the nodding crowd
It is the drums preside, like giant tumours.

To every cocked ear, expert in its greed,
His battered signature subscribes 'No Pope',
The goatskins sometimes plastered with his blood.
The air is pounding like a stethoscope.

"How does that grab youse, eh?" Egbert smiled around at us, "it's very good, isn't it?"

Cedric sneered contemptuously at us all, at Heaney, at the sound of the Lambeg which continued to beat its way into Long Kesh and, of course, at Egbert. "They use pigskin, not goatskin," he retorted. "There's an oul' lad in Sandy Row makes them.

"I used to watch them at it all the time. One Eleventh night I walked the whole length of the Shankill." He paused at our amused and doubting grins. "Nawh . . . Like, it was before the troubles. About 1965. It was safe as a row of houses then."

"That's what has me in here." It was Egbert's turn to sneer. "That's what he told me when he sent me out. 'An easy job,' he told me. 'You'll be as safe as a row of houses,' he said. It's a pity he didn't tell the judge."

We laughed as Cedric, finally needled into silence, glared across at Egbert. Outside the Lambeg continued its primitive tattoo.

"I hear the Loyalist cages are having a Twelfth parade," I volunteered, anxious lest Egbert and Cedric stop talking altogether. "They've got wood an' all gathered in their cage for the Eleventh night. It should be good *craic*."

"Aye," said Egbert, "it'll be quare *craic* all right! I remember when we used to live down the Grosvenor Road all my mates were Orangies. I used to go round with them collecting wood and stuff for the Twelfth bonfires."

"That doesn't surprise me," retorted Cedric. "Your ones probably took the soup as well."

"Yahoo," Your Man laughed, "that's a bit near the bone."

"Wha' d'ye mean?" I asked, hunkering up against the

side of the shower hut and edging out of the sun and into the shade. "Wha' d'ye mean, his ones took the soup."

"They sold their Os for penny rolls and their Macs for bits of hairy bacon," Cedric recited.

"He's trying to say that we Anglicised our names for a bowl of soup and a crust. It's his idea of a joke," said Egbert.

"Ah, don't mind him," Your Man consoled. "He thinks he's descended from the ancient Kings of Ireland."

"So I am. From the King of Ulster."

"With a name like Cedric?" Egbert challenged.

The rest of us smiled. Outside the camp on the Cemetery Road the Lambeg continued its hollow staccato.

"What we need in Ireland is a thirty-two county Ulster," Your Man suggested. Cedric was nonplussed.

"Do youse know what was the most important consequence of the Battle of the Boyne?" he asked.

"No conferring and you have twenty seconds to answer," mimicked Egbert. "Right Magnus?"

Cedric glared at him. "OK, Brains Trust," he said scornfully.

"The thing with the Battle of the Boyne was that the old Gaelic system was finally forced onto its knees, and the Protestant Ascendancy was established by depriving and exploiting everyone else," he continued. "Youse probably think the Boyne and the Twelfth is about religion. It's not: it's about power."

"It's really the First, you know," Egbert interrupted, "the Twelfth took place on the First. I mean, the Battle of the Boyne took place on the first of July, not the twelfth."

"Well the Orangemen like it on the Twelfth. It suits their holidays better," Your Man grinned.

"They don't even know what they're celebrating," sneered Cedric. "D'youse know that the Pope supported King Billy?"

He looked around at us. Your Man handed round a snout tin. While we made roll-ups the sound of the dinner lorry unloading its cargo of goodies at the cage gate drowned out the noise of the Lambeg drum.

"We're on the tap for a bit of home cooking," Big Marshall and Cleaky shouted over to us as they trundled towards the gate to collect the day's rations. "Any of youse get a parcel today?"

"Nawh," Your Man replied, squinting into the sun at them and then back again to Cedric. "Them two's always on the tap," he muttered.

Cedric was unaffected by the distraction. He took a long drag on his cigarette as he continued his narrative.

"It was King Billy and the Pope against King James and the King of France. The Pope paid part of Billy Boy's expenses and when news of his victory at the Boyne reached Rome a *Te Deum* was sung at the Vatican, and there were celebrations in the other main Catholic cities, too."

Cedric looked around at us again. "Look lads, if youse don't believe me read any half-decent history book."

"He's right," Egbert, to our surprise, agreed. "He's right on the button for once. That's what happened."

Cedric looked at him suspiciously. "Aye, but do you know why it happened?"

Before anyone could answer he went on, "Pope Innocent . . ."

"Anything to Paddy Innocent in the half-hut?" Egbert chuckled.

"Pope Innocent," Cedric repeated with only a slight edge to his voice, "Pope Innocent supported the Dutchman, William, against James after the English parliament sacked James and invited William to take on the job. James teamed up with the King of France to try to get his throne back and he and William fought for it in Ireland. The Pope and all the rest wanted to curb the power of France."

"All this history's a bit boring," Your Man yawned.

"It's the way he tells it," said Egbert.

"Do you think that eejit out there beating hell out of his

drum knows all this about the Pope and King Billy?" Your Man mused.

"Nawh. Well, to be honest, I don't know. Like, you didn't know it yourself, did you?"

Your Man nodded his ignorance. Outside the camp the Lambeg continued its rat-a-tat, rat-a-tat, rat-a-tat-tat. Your Man whistled in time to the beat. "But I'm not an Orangeman, am I?" he said eventually.

"That's no excuse for not knowing your own history," Cedric declared in his most professorial tone of voice. "It's no wonder the country's the way it is."

"Awh take a grip of yourself, will ye," Egbert spluttered.

"It's all right," Your Man said, "I'm well used to his slabbering."

"Hold on, hold on," I chided, "take it easy. It's too good a day for arguing."

"I agree," said Cedric loftily. "Youse uns should have a wee bit more come and go in youse."

"My arse," grunted Egbert.

"Ach, c'mon, let it go," Your Man soothed.

"I was going to say," said Cedric, "I was going to say that after the Boyne – the grand alliance between King Billy and the Pope – all religions were banned except the Episcopalian Church."

"You're joking. You're having us on," Egbert exclaimed in disbelief.

"And what's more," Cedric persisted, "religious toleration, among other things, was dropped when the English broke the Treaty of Limerick. Youse uns are good examples of that type of intolerance." He pulled himself to his feet. "Youse can have it," he huffed.

"Ach, come on," Your Man and I pleaded. "Sit down, don't be taking the Nick. Sit down and enjoy the sun."

"Aye, sit down, comrade," Egbert said grudgingly. Cedric hesitated but then sat down again, slowly and peevishly.

"No surrender," hissed Egbert. "Not an inch," he

whispered in disgust. "You're as staunch as a bucket of snow."

"Cedric carry on, carry on with your story," Your Man said quickly and magnanimously.

Cedric started again. Egbert sighed. I settled myself once more in the shade of the shower hut. Your Man stretched himself on the tarmac. Outside the camp on the Blairis Cemetery Road the Lambeg continued its musical monotone, and Cedric went on, and the beating of the drum went on, and the sound of Cedric's voice and the beating of the drum went on. And on. And on. And on.

DOGGONE

Your Man was homesick.

"How many bus-stops are there between Castle Street and Casement Park on the left side of the Falls Road?" he asked.

"That's a trick question," Cedric answered. "Casement Park is on the Andersonstown Road, not the Falls."

Your Man wasn't amused. He was lying on the bottom bunk. Old hands always go for a bottom bunk; that way, when the roof leaks, they avoid drowning. If the fella in the top bunk leaks that's another story. Cedric was in the top bunk and, as I was saying, Your Man wasn't amused by his answer.

"You know what I mean. Stop messing around."

"How do I know what you mean if you don't mean what you say?"

"Take it easy," Egbert butted in. "Youse two are always squabbling. That's no way for comrades to behave towards each other."

"Ach, I'm sick of all youse doing your whack on my back," Your Man muttered, pulling the blanket over his head and exiting from the conversation. "You can't answer a simple question."

"He can't do his own whack," retorted Cedric. "He expects me to count all the bus-stops on the Falls Road. He must think my head's cut."

"You know," said Egbert, "the best bus in the whole world was the last bus up the Whiterock Road on a Saturday night."

"Number eleven!" Your Man's blanket slid back down off his face. "Aye, all human life was on that last bus."

Egbert sat up on the edge of his bunk. "You'd get a sing-song and a fight and a drink and a lumber all on the one journey. Sometimes I thought it wouldn't get up the Whiterock hill; there'd be so many people on it the bus used to sway from side to side. Aye, them were the days. Walking home from the terminus through the Murph ..."

"I'd never walk through the Murph late at night," Your Man interrupted, "not after Herbo's dog was killed."

"Ah, that wouldn't worry me. I saw it one night; heard it too."

They fell silent, each alone with his thoughts.

"Well go on!" Cedric exploded. "What's the story about Herbo's dog? Who is Herbo anyway?"

"Herbo?" Your Man eased himself up on the bunk. "Herbo was a neighbour of mine. A good fellow. He had a dog; it was called Bo. In those days dogs got the same surname as their owner, you know: Snowie McKenna, Patch Gibney, Rover Burns, Spot MacStravick, Rhubarb Hartley. In this case, Bo Gibson. Probably the same nowadays," he mused. "Anyway, during the riots in Ballymurphy, Herbo, like the rest of us, was always in the thick of it and the dog was always with him."

"That dog feared nothing," said Egbert.

"It hated the Brits. Many's the time I saw them giving it a kicking but it still wouldn't give up having a go at them."

"It was a real patriot?" Cedric suggested.

"Nawh, it was an oul' mongrel."

"A real gamester an' all," Your Man continued. "One day there was a big riot in Divismore Park in front of the Brit barracks at the Taggart. Somebody threw a nail bomb. It landed just to the side of a Brit riot squad. Bo was up there in the thick of it as usual. He saw the nail bomb, picked it up in his mouth and, pleased as punch and with his tail wagging, he set off back to Herbo."

"You never saw a crowd scattering like it did that night," Egbert interjected excitedly. "Bo went through them like a knife through butter. All I saw was people leaping over hedges, up garden paths, over fences."

"And Herbo took off like a shot up Glenalina Road with the dog in hot pursuit," Your Man said sadly. "The last I saw of Bo was as he turned the corner of Divismore Park. Herbo was screaming 'Drop it, Bo! Drop it!'"

"Then the nailer exploded," Egbert sighed, "and that was the end of Bo. Later that night we buried him in Herbo's back-garden. The local kids gave him a guard of honour. And Herbo: Herbo was a great mimic. He used to be able to make a noise like a trumpet – he'd blow 'Advance' and 'Retreat' for the rioters during the riots. The night Bo was buried he played the 'Last Post'. It was sad really. He was a great dog."

"That's why I wouldn't walk through the streets late at night. They say Bo can be heard howling – a real ghostly sound – before someone from the Murph gets killed," Your Man said.

"Ach, that's a load of rubbish. That's what the Ballymurphy people tell their kids to make them go to sleep. You shouldn't heed that oul' nonsense," Egbert was adamant.

"You know the Brits dug up Bo's body for forensics," Your Man replied.

"Oh, I didn't know that."

"Aye. The same thing happened to our cat. It . . ."

That's where I left them. It's always like that when Your Man gets homesick. The loose talk starts. It's true about Bo Gibson though. I was there myself. And I'm sure you've guessed the real reason why Your Man won't walk through the Murph late at night. You haven't? Well . . .

Nawh, better not. Let's let sleeping dogs lie.

REMEMBERING A
HEDGEHOG

There was a big house in Huskey's Field. In days long past it was probably the local manse but everyone in Ballymurphy just called it Huskey's. From the Springfield Road a long, tree-lined avenue provided entrance while another more humble path cut from the side of the house towards the river which flowed down from Rock Dam. Perhaps long ago the owners of the dam and the flax-works connected with it lived in the big house. Maybe Huskey knew their history, but no one bothered asking him. When the big house became a school he became its caretaker and when it became an occasional clinic he earned a uniform, and a reputation which he probably didn't deserve.

Huskey's field, you see, was well stocked with chestnut trees and no amount of "Trespassers Will Be Prosecuted" notices could keep us from raiding them during the cheeser season. Nor, indeed, could we be prevented from playing Ralioh, lighting fires, or knocking wood for the 15th of August. Below Huskey's the brickyard held its own fascination, while the Pithead, stretching from behind Beechmount, was a place over which a gang from Westrock (Tintown) held an uneasy reign. Rival gangs from the Rock and the Murph provided consistent, if unorthodox opposition to Tintown's supremacy, while Durango, an RUC speed-cop, messed everyone about equally as he chased combatants, often mounted on stolen gypsy ponies, if and when they strayed out of the area.

On Mondays, Wednesdays and Fridays queues formed at Huskey's for rations of cod-liver oil, orange juice and milk tokens. They came from Ballymurphy, across the wee bridge at Divismore Park and up through the cheeser trees. Local protests led to the building of a new clinic on the Springfield Road, beside the entrance to the long avenue, and after that workmen arrived to cut down the chestnut trees. Pipes were laid alongside the river and rumours of a new RUC barracks being built in Huskey's swept the area. They didn't build an RUC barracks, though; they built Springhill, and as a small group of warehouses crept from opposite Whiterock Orange Hall to envelope the Pithead, and as Curry's Timber Yard climbed up over the Brickie, the new estate emerged from the gripwork and brown muck of Huskey's. Grey, barrack-like houses replaced the cheeser trees and a memory of the tree-lined avenue was retained in name, if not in deed, by Springhill Avenue, the only street of any length among the rabbit's warren of entries and alleyways.

In 1971 while thinking all these thoughts I walked through the Whiterock towards Ballymurphy. It was about one o'clock in the morning. The Paras were garrisoned in the area but we usually got plenty of warning from the local people as to their whereabouts, so I strolled along letting my thoughts wander with me. Coming along Westrock Drive I noticed a small bundle huddled close to the kerb on the road beside me. You probably won't believe this, but there I was a few seconds later, kneeling on the road face to face with . . . a hedgehog. I got pretty excited, never having met a real live hedgehog before, so I pulled off my anorack and with much caution lest I was bitten or, even worse, speared by one of its spines, I edged it into my clothy container and headed for some safe refuge. Bridget's was the nearest and most obvious place, so I cut across the gardens, close to where the cheeser trees had once stood and Huskey's – for all they had done to it – didn't seem so far away.

To my dismay, however, no one in Bridget's shared my excitement. They had tolerated me long enough so they weren't surprised to see me arriving as I did, in the middle of their session, shirt-sleeved and with a destitute hedgehog wrapped up in my jacket. But they were not amused, and Bridget gave off about fleas as I deposited my prickly friend on her sofa; only Dorothy, the daughter of the house, was at all interested in my story. Bridget's was one of those houses – an aluminium bungalow, in fact – in which neighbours gathered for a late-night bingo session and a bit of *craic*. I had disrupted all this and I suffered as a result.

"What are you going to do with that?" asked a girl, who, incidentally, I later married.

"I'm going to set it free," I declared.

"If the Paras catch you it'll look good in the papers," Bridget threw in: 'Charged with possession of a hedgehog'." The neighbours laughed, I took a redener and the hedgehog rolled itself up even tighter.

"Well, I'm going to have to do something with it," I said lamely.

"You're not leaving it here," Bridget warned, "a dirty oul' thing like that. Throw it over Corrigan Park wall. That's probably where it came from."

"The Brits use Corrigan at night," Dorothy said. "Look, it's stretching itself out!" she exclaimed.

And so it was. A small, wet, pig-like snout and two bright, intelligent eyes had emerged from the bundle of prickles on the sofa as the hedgehog adjusted to the heat in Bridget's front room.

"He's making himself comfortable," someone declared.

"Are we going to get on with our game?" another more

crabbit neighbour moaned. "Take him out of that and let's get on with our bingo."

"C'mon into the back," Dorothy suggested to me. "Here, you carry it." So into the back we went.

"Flip me," I complained, "I'm always in trouble. What am I going to do?"

"Take it to Riddel's Field. I'll watch out for the Brits for you and it will only take us a minute anyway. We could skite up and down before me Ma knows we're away," Dorothy whispered excitedly. "C'mon, if we don't leave it somewhere safe the dogs'll ate lumps out of it. No use sitting there with a big long face on you. I'll switch off the lights and we can sneak out." And so we sneaked out.

Back we went along the way I had walked earlier, across the bungalows and into the 'Rock, where we visited Mrs Crowe's for a few minutes, and then off again with Dorothy willing the Brits away from us and me nervous in the now deserted streets with their dark, sleeping houses. On till we got to the Giant's Foot. A minute later I was up and over the gap in the wall and the hedgehog was dumped amid the undergrowth along the outskirts of the field. I returned a little breathless to Dorothy and together we hurried back towards her mother's. The excitement was over and our journey home seemed longer and sillier with every shadow we passed. "If I get caught I'll kill you, wee girl," I hissed.

"You'll be all right," she laughed. "You're always gurning about something. You wouldn't have wanted your stupid hedgehog killed, would you? Sure, here we are, home again. I told you it would be easy. They probably didn't even miss us."

And they didn't. We told them but they thought we were stupid, and they were right of course. Getting caught for the sake of a hedgehog would have been as thick as champ. At least I thought so. Dorothy didn't. She reckoned it was sound. "After all," she exclaimed, "you couldn't let the poor wee thing die, now could you?"

A few short months later Dorothy herself was dead.

She and Maura, her older sister, heard of a Brit raid in the Falls while they were at a party. They rushed off in a friend's car to warn the people there. A Brit patrol opened fire on the car and killed the two sisters. It was early in the morning, a morning just like the one we spent bringing the hedgehog to safety. And Dorothy, who had grown up near Huskey's Field, became the first volunteer soldier of Cumann na mBan to be killed by British troops. Bridget Maguire lost her two daughters, and myself and the girl I later married lost a friend.

Anytime I think of Huskey's Field, of Westrock, the Murph, Springhill, the Giant's Foot, or of hedgehogs, I think of Dorothy. She was nineteen. She will be five years dead next month. You wouldn't think it was as long ago as that. Isn't it strange how Long Kesh sharpens memories like these?

Dorothy Maguire and Maura Meehan were shot dead by the British Army on 23 October 1971.

PIGEONS

It all started in June. A pigeon landed on the hut roof when we were in Cage Four. Cricky, Dicky and Johnny got her to land on the ground between the huts, walked her into a corner and then, with great skill, they grabbed hold of her. She was exhausted, hungry and in bad health, so they built a wee box, kept her warm and fed and doctored her until she was fit and well again. Up until this a pigeon to me had always been a pigeon. I was to discover that there are pigeons and . . . well, there are pigeons.

This particular invalid was a lady pigeon, a dark checkered hen, in fact, and as she wasn't really herself for a while I used to nip over to Johnny's locker and take the odd blimp at her. Johnny didn't mind, Cricky was positively bursting with information and Dicky made tea. I soon learned all kinds of things about pigeons in general and about this checkered hen-pigeon in particular.

A few weeks later ourselves and our feathered friend moved out of Cage Four and we were only back in this cage a wee while when a second pigeon arrived. He flew into one of the wash-houses in another cage and the lads passed him down to Cricky, Dicky and Johnny. Great interest was created in the cage when we, and our black checkered hen, discovered that this was no ordinary pigeon. He was, in fact, a gentleman pigeon; a cock-pigeon and a red checkered cock-pigeon to boot. The plot began to thicken because, after a good feed, a drink and plenty of rest, he soon let us know that we were now in the company of a mammy pigeon and a daddy pigeon.

The box wasn't good enough any longer so it was decided that a shed would have to be built. The lads set to work and soon there was a pretty sound wee shed in the corner of the study hut. The two pigeons were installed and they quickly settled in. The study hut, incidentally, does service as the chapel, the library, a centre for discussions, lectures and staff meetings, somewhere to iron clothes, as a rehearsal room for our budding Christy Moores and Sean O Riadas, a bolt-hole to hide away when big Ds settle in and, of course, as a place where I slip off to scribble these lines. The pigeons didn't seem to mind all this activity. They ignored remarks from curious clergymen and commenced to play a diversionary role in lectures, discussions and staff meetings.

The third pigeon arrived shortly after the shed was built. She was a bronze, pied hen who landed, completely knackered, on the watch-tower just outside our cage. Cricky, Dicky and Johnny put our other two birds out on the study-hut roof and the bronze hen flew down to them. After an hour of coaxing, whistling and cooing, Cricky got her down onto the ground and in beneath the study hut. All the lads crowded around the hut and after some urgent crawling, shooing and shouting they finally managed to get hold of her. The poor frightened bird was in a bad state and the lads kept her well away from the other pigeons. Cricky, Dicky and Johnny thought she might not last the night so they stayed up nursing her with a supply of medicine which they made up themselves. The following morning she was as right as rain and the three exhausted but happy Samaritans put her in with the other birds.

The fourth pigeon dropped in at the end of August. He landed on the canteen roof and refused to budge. After informing the more ignorant POWs that this was nothing less than a mealy cock, our three friends sent the desirable and highly sensual dark checkered hen up to have a word with him. After a bit of provocative strutting and cooing she flew back to the study-hut roof and the gullible oul' mealy cock flew after her. We now had two mammy pigeons and, as you'll have guessed, two daddy pigeons.

Food became a problem as proper pigeon corn couldn't be got anywhere. Working on the principle that hunger is a good sauce, the boys improvized with a mixture of brown bread and budgie seed. After some initial footering about, our cocks and hens started gobbling it up and, as Paul's budgies became noticeably thinner, the pigeons became remarkably plump. At that point they commenced flying. Cricky, Dicky and Johnny co-ordinated the take-offs and landings and POWs assembled daily in the yard to watch progress and compare flying styles.

The birds, delighted with their audience, kited, pivoted, swooped and fluttered, climbing up and dropping down again. As Your Man remarked, "They used up the whole sky". Then they started to go off on their own, and anxious hours were spent scanning the horizon and peering off across the skyline. As they returned, tired and contented, sometimes together, sometimes straggling in alone, Cricky, Dicky and Johnny whistled them down and laid out clean drinking water and fresh brown bread with budgie seed. By this time the lads were talking of wee younkers and nesting boxes were installed in the pigeon shed. As our colony of flying birds increased to eight, Cricky, Dicky and Johnny scrubbed and mopped the shed every day while the less patient among us checked anxiously for eggs or signs of eggs-to-be.

Then the screws took the shed down. It was during a raid and luckily the birds had flown off, as the screws (with us locked safely in the canteen) began to demolish their wee home. The pigeons now had no landmark to guide them back to our cage and in those few days of bad weather three were lost. One, a white squealer, had disappeared a few days previously and only four returned after their shed was wrecked. The Governor said they could be used to send messages. This idiotic assertion was dismissed by Cricky who explained, as everyone knows, that you have to take pigeons away to release them before they can come home with a message.

Since the raid we just stick a board out of the study-hut window, and the pigeons fly off when the screw raiding parties arrive and return when they depart. Last week another blue checkered hen arrived from Madra's sanctuary in Cage Ten and yesterday Cage Thirteen sent down a sick, black-checkered cock.

And so the pigeons remain, perched on tables, on the smoothing iron, dozing under chairs, and generally happy and contented among the bric-a-brac in our study hut. They fly off each morning, off over the camp to some special place of their own. They return each evening and, despite the loss of their shed and apart from their present discomforts, Cricky, Dicky and Johnny look after them well. In fact, they are far better off, Your Man says, than the rest of us mere humans in Cage Eleven. Cedric disagrees and Egbert doesn't care either way. As long as they aren't stoolie-pigeons they're welcome, he says, which is more than he ever conceded about the rest of us.

CHRISTIANS FOR FREEDOM?

I met Bishop Philbin once. He and British Army supremo Tony Dyball were on one side of a barricade in Bread Street off the Falls Road in Belfast in August 1969, and myself and a motley crew of long-haired hooligans were on the other side. The good Mr Dyball wanted the barricades down and Dr Philbin had been brought in to speak to the natives. Unfortunately, we and he spoke different languages so, after some mutual abuse had been exchanged, he departed in high dudgeon and the poor natives were left to face the British Army bulldozers – alone.

I did try to meet Dr Philbin again after that, of course. Not wanting the odd barricade to come between me and the hierarchy, I journeyed to the palace (methinks that's the proper jargon) to discuss the affairs of Ballymurphy with him. This pilgrimage of mine followed his sudden and unfounded attack on the people of our estate. Unfortunately, I wasn't permitted an audience and had to content myself with the sight of Ballymurphy mothers handing in a letter of protest to the apprentice priest who peeked out at them from behind the Bishop's door. Ah, those were the days.

I nearly met Cardinal Conway twice. The first time was when I was visiting big Joe McCann's home on the Glen

Road. The Cardinal also happened to be visiting that day. Visiting his mother, that is, but as she lived next-door you could say our paths crossed. Well, at least I cast a disdainful look at the ecclesiastical limousine which parked itself across my path. I saw nothing of its owner.

The same thing almost happened in Cage Twenty-Two. I was seated on the toilet one day, bowed down with matters of theological interest, when the Cardinal was shepherded past by a crusade of curates. We never got within smelling distance of each other and, having a more important matter in hand, so to speak, I and he passed our respective ways, unchallenged.

And now, dear reader, after that lengthy preamble we come to the nitty-gritty. I only wanted you to know that I have had some experience, in the near past, with Church dignatories. I wouldn't like this to be seen as yet another anti-clerical statement from a disgruntled Republican. God only knows who reads this stuff.

Let me state my case briefly. It is my contention as a lay member of the Catholic Church, that the hierarchy of that Church have been found somewhat lacking in their contribution and in their attitudes to the resolution of the situation in which we find ourselves. I am not alone in my thinking. Many other people, more worthy than myself, have made the same assertions these last few years. The case is a simple one. It is that the Catholic Church has failed miserably to fulfill its role in Ireland.

This is nothing new, of course. History tells its own story of the pro-establishment line adopted by Church leaders throughout the ages. The Catholic Church in Ireland is traditionally conservative, inward looking and, for historical reasons, in a position of some power and influence in Irish affairs. The Church perhaps fulfilled its Christian role best in St Patrick's time and during the Penal Days. Since then, with only a few notable exceptions, it has deserted the poor.

The Church's attitude on certain issues makes things rather confusing for the layperson and it is my belief that the apathy of Church leaders on matters of national, social and economic importance have led to a widening gap between the Church and the people. You see, the present generation cannot identify with the hierarchy and the hierarchy doesn't identify with them, and without identification you have only isolation. As a result, Church leaders are increasingly becoming part of the problem and less and less a part of the solution.

Their lack of imaginative thinking is typified by the Irish bishops in their Joint Pastoral letter, "Human Life is Sacred". I secured a copy of it and, dear brethren and sistren, it falls far short of the analysis that such a subject requires. Fr Camille Torres, in his interpretation of the Papal Encylical, "Populorum Proggressio", does more to expound Christian teaching than all the bishops put together. Indeed, the Pastoral Letter from the Third World, "Gospel and Revolution", puts them all to shame.

And so, what is the point in my devoting myself to this subject? Well, for one thing, it's because I'm interested in these things and, for another, the churches are one of the prime moulders of public (and perhaps private, who knows?) opinion, standards and attitudes. But, primarily, it's because within the grassroots I think a change is coming. Unfortunately this change, or at least public debate about the churches' role, seems to be confined to the Catholic Church.

Some may think, perhaps, that this subject is not suitable material for a Republican, but surely in our new Ireland there will also be hierarchies and our attitudes must be in step with people's thinking, geared to their spiritual as well as social needs.

For all these reasons it is important that Republicans (whether Catholic, Protestant or Pagan) keep in touch with the present debate sparked off, yet again, by Fr Desmond Wilson. You must all be aware of his viewpoints, his attitudes and his denunciations of the hierarchies, so perhaps I could put before you some viewpoints from other hard-working people's priests.

Fr James McDyer states baldly: "Christianity was a revolution of the left. I think we are not being true to the Christian ethic by our fantastic private enterprise philosophy. I would go so far as to say that capitalism in its worst sense, carried to its logical end, is the antithesis of Christianity. Socialism, carried to its logical conclusion, is complementary to Christianity."

Fr Joe McVeigh declares: "The real issues that are raised by the conflict at grassroots level are about 1. the continuous harassment of people by security forces; 2. the treatment of people who are arrested and in prison; 3. the problems of no jobs, job insecurity, bad housing and the increasing scarcity of money; 4. the control and operation of education; 5. the moral and spiritual formation of young people; 6. the distribution and ownership of land, property and resources; 7. the problem of mixed marriages.

"Sometimes one would think that as far as the churches are concerned the only problem in Ireland is 'the men of violence'. There has been very little compassion for the many people caught up in the web of physical violence. There has been little effort to show any non-violent way of bringing about change in society. The Gospel is a radical message with something to say to the specific problems I mention above, compassion to the oppressed, not to the oppressor at all times."

An tAth. Piaras Ó Dúill asks, "Is there really a war [in Ireland] and is it a just one or not? Personally I do think there is a war and the question is of how just it is or not. There is no point in evading these issues by issuing a blanket condemnation without thinking about it. A blanket condemnation of violence is not something that is really helpful at the moment. Institutionalized violence of the kind we have seen in the North is just as bad and has to be eradicated before we can look at the rest."

Fr Faul states: "tortures of prisoners clearly violate the United Nations Declaration of Human Rights, and their standard minimum rules for the treatment of prisoners, as well as the Second Vatican Constitution of the Church of the Modern World, Pat 27. Any of these actions inflicted on a person is an assault constituting actual bodily harm or grievous bodily harm. It breaks the law of the land."

And on another occasion Fr Faul says, "If prison conditions are designed and the regime is implemented in such a way that men's characters are deformed through repression, then the situation is immoral."

These then are some statements which receive less publicity than those expounded by Bishops Daly, Philbin, Casey, or Cardinal Conway. Even Bishop Newman, who may disagree with some of the above quotes, but who was courageous enough to call for a British withdrawal, was met by a deafening silence from his fellow dignitories. He spoke alone.

MOLES

The Derry wans were talking about Derry. About the Bog,
the Creggan and Shantallow. Your Man beside me
smirked and burst into a chorus of "Danny Boy" as he
slid down off the roof where we had been taking our ease
and more than our share of sunshine.

I pull myself to my feet and gaze around at Long Kesh.
Cage upon cage stretches away in every direction. Black
tarred roofs and grey metallic ones; black roofs where
new cages have replaced those burnt out and grey ones
where work has yet to begin. Away to my right the
motorway shimmers in the bright sunshine and behind it
green fields climb backwards to meet the horizon. The
odd farmhouse dots the landscape and a whitewashed
church sits comfortably between us and the motorway.
The British Army posts frown down on us and nearer at
hand screws' watch-towers roast in the heat. Cars and
lorries whizz up and down the M1. Two new Brit posts
monitor the open ground between the perimeter fence
and the motorway itself. That's where Hugh Coney was
shot. Out there, between us and them; between Long
Kesh and freedom; between motorway and concentration
camp.

Did you ever dig a tunnel? Down into a shaft. A makeshift trap-door overhead and then in. In, into clay and

gravel and rocks and water, everywhere seeping water, and the pitch blackness and bad nerves making bad air taste worse.

"A good trap's the thing," say the experts. "You must have a good trap-door or you're lost."

We lost quite a few times but then we were only amateurs. Cage Five was the place for tunnels. They had them everywhere, but one by one they were discovered. Screws fell down them while patrolling the yard, tunnels collapsed and men were dragged back from clutching clay and clinging gravel. They used to call Cage Five "The Moles". Other cages had tunnels too, of course, where internees and sentenced men worked hard towards perimeter fences and freedom. But up in Cage Five, nearer the fences, boggers rarely stopped push, push, pushing and soon below ground the cage must have been a maze of half-finished tunnels.

Hugh was shot coming out of a tunnel. You don't hear much about it now and it's not even a year yet. Just after the fire it was. There were tunnels in cages Four, Two and Five, and only for the distance they would have been going in all the cages. But Cage Two's collapsed and then Cage Four's. They filled the shafts in again so the screws wouldn't find them. Hard work, after digging muck out, to have to put it back again, but nobody complained. It had to be done because loose talk being loose talk, everyone knew that Cage Five must still be going.

These were pretty good days. All around us Long Kesh lay razed to the ground. Everyone sprouting beards and everyone and everything bogging with dirt. Paddy the Lad, rummaging through twisted timbers and finding souvenirs for all who wanted them. Men sleeping in the open or, like the most of us, in makeshift huts and shelters. Sing-songs at night and concerts. Paddy B singing "Mule Train" and "The Music Man". I wet myself one night listening to him singing "The Music Man". And Big Dominic and Billy R conducting campfire style sing-alongs.

No visits, no parcels and few letters getting out, but up in Cage Five digging, digging, digging. I wasn't there myself but the stories came back. Stories of flooding and collapsing, of no shoring and "bad air". Of "It's stopped, it's finished," and then: "It's started again! I wonder will they make it? We're bound to get a raid some day now, you know. It must be tight by this time." And it was, part of it under water and long twists in it to avoid obstacles, and the air must have been stinking.

We didn't know it was through until we heard the shooting. Out there it was, away to the right, between us and the M1. Between Long Kesh and freedom. We were just walking around our cage when the self-loading rifle spat out its message. We stopped for an instant. "It must be Cage Five. They've shot somebody. Head for Cage Four. Mess up the head count. Move!"

Then the long night. After the first charge which took us through the wire and over into Cage Four; after the stomach-wrenching CR gas; after the doubt, the uncertainty and the rumours; after all the digging and toiling. After everything.

"One man has been shot dead in Long Kesh." The half-seven news with its impersonal message, the message from outside brought into us on a transistor radio. "This is the end of this news bulletin."

Sin é. One dead. A Brit soldier dispensing justice from the muzzle of his SLR. Lying out between us and freedom, weapon cocked, safety off, waiting for us. One POW dead or dying. Long Kesh in the news again. Hugh Coney, IRA volunteer and internee, shot dead. Out there, away to my right.

Out there close to the motorway that he was trying to reach. Out there where the cars and lorries whizz up and down the M1, past the whitewashed church, past Long Kesh, past Cage Five, past reality.

I lie back on the roof and gaze skywards. That's the only way to get a long-distance look in Long Kesh. All the horizons here are artificial, barbed-wire ones. You can't see any distance at all, except skywards. So I gaze at the distant sky and think of other escape efforts.

The tunnel from Cage Seven was inching its way towards the perimeter fence. It headed, at a worm's pace, towards the area where the H-Blocks now stand; by Big Ned's reckoning it was eighty-foot long. In Cage Eight a shorter tunnel was started in the grass verge. It only had to cover thirty-odd feet but as it was being worked in the open, right under the screws' noses, progress was much slower. In Cage Twenty-Two as well a shaft was sunk, and the men began to edge along underground in an effort to join with the others.

Digging tunnels isn't much *craic*. In fact it's scary, because even in summer it's difficult to stay above the water level. Dry digging is impossible and constant seepage makes sudden shifts in the ground inevitable. Even the shoring is unreliable and prone to collapse at the slightest touch. The water seeps in everywhere because Long Kesh is built on a bog.

The name itself comes from *Ceis Fhada* which translates from Gaelic as "the long ditch" or "basket". Even the new Brit term, The Maze, comes from the Irish *An Má* – the plain. Methinks it should have been called *An tUisce* – the water. At any rate, for all these reasons, I've always avoided going down tunnels. I was perfectly willing to bale out water, hide dirt, wash clothes, clean up, cut shoring, make tools or keep watch. I was even prepared to undertake the awesome job of digging through two feet of concrete floor with only the most basic of home-made chisels. Anything as long as I didn't actually have to go up the tunnel. And, anyway, I was no good at digging.

None of this made any difference, of course, because orders is orders. They say you can ask questions afterwards.

Afterwards?

So there I was, feeling foolish in a pair of shorts, letting on to be indifferent to the death that surely awaited me. Joking casually to Your Man. There was no way out of it.

Your Man went down first, disappearing slowly as the shaft swallowed him up. I followed reluctantly, feet first. Things got a bit tight when I was waist-deep in the floor. There wasn't enough room to get my arms through so I forced my body into position forty-four (yoga, of course) and then down I slid.

There were two inches of water at the base of the shaft, cold water which lapped in little waves around my ankles. The tunnel mouth was only two feet square and as I hunkered down I could see it narrowing as bags of returned dirt bellied their way out from the sides. Your Man's feet, toe-deep in silt, glared back at me as I resignedly began my journey.

We were soon hard at work. Slow, tortuous work. He scraped at the face with a makeshift shovel and I lay on his legs, holding him steady, doing my best to minimize movement. Wishing I was somewhere else. We were only down for twenty minutes. I think I could have stuck it longer, lying there petrified, but then suddenly Your Man let off one of his great, slow, strangled farts. I don't want to make it sound melodramatic, but in that cramped space, far below Long Kesh's tarmacked and concreted surface, I panicked. Well, I think that's why I panicked. In any case, it was as good, as original and as believable an excuse as any other, so we shuffled our way backwards towards the shaft and the abnormality overhead.

They never let me go down again. Nobody said anything, of course. They just put me to hiding dirt. I looked disappointed, suspected Your Man of back-stabbing, and offered a silent prayer of thanksgiving to St Jude.

In the meantime things continued above and below ground and by the end of the second week we were feeling pretty hopeful. Cage Seven had almost reached the perimeter, Eight had survived a heavy fall of rain, and we had scraped through two British Army raids. The Beard and Wee Owen were even planning a holiday in France; Cedric had sent all his clothes out, and Your Man talked of the propaganda that his return to the struggle would warrant. I thought quietly to myself of the safety of west Mayo and spoofed along with the rest.

On Saturday we were moved. No warning or advance notice from the prison regime. We tried to talk our way out of it, of course, but you know the score yourself. There's a hard way and an easy way; you move or the Brits move you. We moved. As a sort of consolation we left our gaping hole in the floor unmarked and unhidden with a note for the head of prison security poking out of its mouth. That at least would get somebody into trouble – the screws are supposed to stop us digging, you see.

Our second day back here saw the start of another tunnel. The one in Seven looked a sure thing and none of us wanted to be left behind. We didn't get as far this time, of course. The shaft was only finished when it was caught. Cage Eight's collapsed a few days later. It nearly killed the screw who disappeared into it.

And the one in Cage Seven? The water got it. It filled up to the ceiling one night along its complete hundred-feet length. It was bound to happen: winter is no time to dig. The heavy rainfall turns the ground into silt and apart from anything else it's a devil to hide.

Now, the summer's different. Your Man reckons that if we just keep below the hardcore we should be OK. He thinks we can manage to stay above water-level that way; if we hit clay we'd be flying. The thing to do is to keep at it. Like, we've nothing else to do anyway, have we?

HARVEY

The Dark broke first.

"For God's sake," he hissed, "somebody shut him up!"

"Shut him up yourself," somebody replied. "Lying there giving your orders. Who do you think you are?"

"Shhh!" Cedric commanded. "Listen."

It was three o'clock in the morning. The hut was bathed in an orange glow from the searchlights outside on the cage wire. From the shadows which enveloped Egbert's bottom bunk we could hear a series of low grunts, high-pitched squeals and irregularly pitched moans. These sounds seemed to grow in volume and intensity and I, for one, listened with increasing dread as the strangely inhuman noises rose to a climax. They seemed to fill the entire hut. I was terrified.

"Jesus, Mary and holy Saint Joseph!" The Dark's plea came from beneath his blankets, as his hand groped below the bed for a boot. Cedric beat him to it. His size ten Doctor Martin's bounced off Your Man's prostrate form. He sat bolt upright.

"Wha', what's up? Where am I?"

"In your granny's. Where do you think you are? Catch yourself on! Keeping everybody awake," the Dark shouted at him.

"That's enough," Cedric cut in.

111

Cedric was our new Hut OC. Our last one had surrendered in the face of protracted undermining by Egbert and Your Man. He had broken like a plate. That's why Cedric got the position; the Cage Staff had decreed that it should rotate around the hut, and Cedric was first. So he came down heavy on Your Man and the Dark: nobody was going to break him.

"The next man to open his mouth is on punishment," he threatened.

"I have to turn on the lights," Your Man said. "I'm not well."

"Don't turn on the bloody lights," the Dark snapped.

"I'll give the orders around here," Cedric reminded him.

He shuffled across the floor and switched on the lights. The Dark sulked further beneath his blankets; we could hear him muttering to himself. Meanwhile Cedric approached Your Man's bunk.

"Gee, you really aren't well," he declared.

And he wasn't; anyone could see that. Your Man's face was putty white and bathed in sweat. With hair plastered to his forehead, his eyes stared out at us, owl-like, from beneath the shadows of his eyebrows.

"I had an awful nightmare," he said. "I dreamed somebody was sitting on my chest, trying to stop me breathing. It was terrible."

"It's your bad conscience," the Dark's blanket suggested.

"That's enough," Cedric insisted. "Lights out in one minute. And you," he pointed to Your Man, "no more messing about. Get to sleep. You'll be all right in the morning."

But he wasn't. He was as pale as death. His eyes were red-rimmed with lack of sleep, he wouldn't eat and he was reeking with sweat. His tongue was OK though. All through the day we heard the story of his encounter with the midnight visitor.

"Too many dirty books," the Dark commented.

"Too much ouija board," Cedric decided. "From now on it's banned."

It made no difference. That night we had a repeat performance, only this time it was Sammy Molloy. Low, strangled half-groans interspersed with sharp intakes of breath and loud thuds as he rolled his head from side to side on the pillow startled us into semi-awakeness in the early hours of the morning.

"If that noise doesn't stop *now* everyone one of youse is on punishment," Cedric thundered. "Youse are like wee children."

"It's not us!" a dozen voices snapped back at him.

Somebody laughed, and then we all froze into a frightened, silent, rigid stillness as a fiendish wail tortured its way free from Sammy's bunk.

"YaaaaAAAAHHH," it howled and then, as we lay petrified, Sammy himself dived from his bed and rolled across the hut floor. "YAAAAAHHHH," he wailed.

The next day Cedric sent for the priest. In the meantime, three men moved out of the hut and the screws asked the Cage OC for a meeting. Apparently the night shift had heard the previous night's ruckus and they had seen our hut lights going on and staying on all night until dawn. The Cage OC came back from his meeting with the screws with a long, serious face on him. He and Cedric had a summit meeting in the drying hut. Afterwards they sent for Your Man and then Sammy. Your Man turned up for the appointment but Sammy refused to leave his bunk, so they adjourned the meeting, put all of us into the yard and reconvened their summit at the foot of Sammy's bunk.

We talked to Cedric later that evening. He was totally noncommittal on his morning's deliberations with the OC and their conversation with Sammy and Your Man. We put him into Coventry. Your Man was more forthcoming.

"Apparently," he confided, "we have a malevolent spirit in our midst. Some diabolical, devil-like, demoniacal lost soul."

"You don't seem too concerned," I observed.

"Ah, but that's 'cos it won't visit me again."

That evening two more men moved out of the hut. The rest of us sat up all night. Nothing happened.

"Any sign of Harvey, lads?" Shoulders O'Doherty shouted over to us the next morning from Cage Twelve.

"What do you mean, Harvey?" Egbert replied.

"You know: the big white rabbit that was in the film with James Stewart. Nobody but James Stewart ever saw it, but I hear it's in your hut now. When did it get sentenced?"

We ignored him. That night Harvey came back again. He overturned a table, pulled the blankets off Cleaky's bed, half-smothered Paddy A and sat on Egbert's chest. We thought Egbert was dying. He didn't react like the others. He just gurgled for about three minutes, with his eyes open and rolling in his head. Then he went deadly quiet.

The priest arrived that afternoon. He listened to all of us and took notes in a wee black book. Then he and the Cage OC went off for a meeting with the Prison Governor.

"I hear Harvey is the ghost of a British Airman who was killed in a plane crash during the last war," Cedric informed us. "Long Kesh used to be an airfield," he added.

By now there were only seven of us left in the hut; eight if you count Harvey.

"What's the priest say?"

"I dunno but he's fairly serious looking."

"The Catholic Church accepts the existence of astral bodies like Harvey," Your Man told us. "They're known as poltergeists. The Church takes a benign attitude about their existence."

"It's a pity it hasn't the same attitude to Republicans," Egbert snorted, but without his usual vehemence.

The priest arrived back about an hour later. He went into our hut on his own. He was there for fifteen minutes. Your Man duked in and said he saw him lying on the floor on his back, kicking and punching at the air and all the time praying in a frenzied, guttural way.

We've never had any trouble since. No sign of Harvey. He's on the missing list, thanks be to God. All the rakers and reprobates who deserted us are back in the hut again. And Cedric's still the OC. The ouija board is still banned.

You probably don't believe a word of this. You don't? I don't blame you; only I witnessed it myself I'd be the same. The attendances at Mass here increased for a while and of course you'll have heard about the Dark's hair. Aye, it went as white as snow. He's very self-conscious about it. That's why we don't talk about Harvey too much. Well, it's one of the reasons I think each of us took a decision to try to forget it. An impossible task but you know what I mean: it's better not to brood on it.

It all came back to me this morning, though, when I saw Shoulders O'Doherty. He was being taken out of Cage Twelve by his OC, the priest and two screws. They took him to the prison hospital. He's over there yet. A medical screw tells me he sits up all night talking to himself.

"Oh, and somebody called Harvey," the screw added. "He's probably working his ticket."

"I wouldn't be too sure about that," I replied, half to myself.

He looked at me strangely.

"I'm serious," I repeated. "I wouldn't dismiss it so easily."

And I wouldn't. Not after the way the Dark's hair went.

FRANK STAGG, 1976

Britain's Ambassador to Chile, Mr Reginald Seconde, said yesterday that he knew that Sheila Cassidy, detained in Chile for fifty-nine days for helping a wounded Chilean guerilla, had been tortured by Santiago police two weeks after her arrest last November. Mr Seconde was reporting to the British Foreign Office after his recall from Chile, and pressure is building up on British Foreign Secretary Jim Callaghan to take some firm action against Chile over the treament of Dr Cassidy. The case has received immense publicity in the British news media and English politicians have been making angry noises against, and about, the use of torture on political prisoners.

At the same time Roy Walsh and two of his comrades are in their third month of solitary confinement in the Prison Segregation Unit (Special Control Unit) of Wormwood Scrubs after their protest there last November. Most Republican prisoners in England are held under solitary confinement conditions and Paul Holmes, in particular, has spent most of his time in the Segregation Unit of Parkhurst Prison, known among Republican POWs as "The Hole". For the past few weeks Frank Stagg, a Republican POW in Wakefield Prison, has been on hunger and thirst strike for one basic demand, and that is a transfer to Ireland so that he may serve his sentence

nearer home. The precedent for this move was established
when Dolours and Marion Price were transferred after a
long and horrifying hunger strike and, again, when Hugh
Feeney and Gerry Kelly were moved to Long Kesh.
Loyalist prisoners, albeit without hunger strike, have also
been transferred, and British soldiers on criminal charges
are brought back to England as a matter of course.

Within the next week or two support for Frank Stagg
will build among the freedom-loving people of Ireland.
This may be too late. It must be stressed that Frank Stagg
will die if pressure is not brought to bear on the Brits
immediately. With this horrible eventuality in mind I
decided to write about conditions for Republican POWs in
English goals, so that while we go about our daily business, at work or at home, each and every one of us may
understand the daily hell which our prisoners in England
are fighting against. To assist me in this I asked two
comrades, Hugh Feeney and Gerry Kelly, to scribble brief
outlines of their experiences so that I could describe Frank
Stagg's prison "routine". Their notes arrived in this cage
this evening and I have used them below almost as they
were written. There is no martyr complex in the following
notes, no talk of doing "bird", no self-pity. As a Republican
prisoner myself, one who has spent a few years in Long
Kesh and a month or two on the Maidstone prison ship, I
have often felt quite sorry for myself and many times I
have had the audacity to feel chuffed at enduring it all.

Since reading Gerry and Hugh's account of force-
feeding I have stopped kidding myself. My two brief
punishment sessions on the boards here, the odd beating-
up on Brit raids, and the conditions which my visitors
endure have all paled into insignificance beside the plight
of our people in England. Long Kesh, Magilligan,
Armagh, Crumlin, Portlaoise, the Curragh, the "Joy" and
Limerick gaols are bad. But prisons in Britain are worse
and are, in truth and fact, living hell-holes.

This ill-treatment must be stopped before Frank Stagg
dies, alone in his prison cell. Frank has been on four

previous hunger strikes and the conditions he is suffering at present are as they were when he was on hunger strike and in solitary confinement in Parkhurst and Long Lartin. He is now in the hospital wing of Wakefield Prison, under the "care" of people who have force-fed Irish prisoners. They call force-feeding "tube" feeding. Frank Stagg may be in the hospital wing, but a prison hospital cannot, in any way, be equated with a civilian hospital. In fact, Frank has been moved from one cell of the prison punishment block to a greater punishment; he still remains in complete solitary confinement, and he must inevitably face force-feeding again. Even after the decision by the British Medical Association to condemn it, force-feeding has not been stopped. British Home Affairs Minister Roy Jenkins, in a reply a few months ago in the House of Commons, stated that he had left the decision to the prison doctor. If, as is likely, Frank Stagg is force-fed again he will suffer the following torture and, because his throat and stomach in particular cannot have healed properly, his health will deteriorate more quickly than it is doing at present.

He will face at least one and maybe two "feedings" daily. Force-feeding is always brutal. No matter how often it occurs the victim does not get used to it. If the "feedings" are not at regular times each day, and usually they are not, then he spends his entire day trying to prepare himself emotionally, trying to restock his determination to fight.

A team of screws are the first to appear. They come into the cell with varying expressions on their faces, ranging from snarls, through impassive indifference, to sheepish, apologetic smiles. Frank will either be "fed" in his cell or dragged outside into another one where he will be held in a bed or on a chair. Usually six or eight screws are involved. They swoop in a planned manner, holding and pressing down on arms and legs. Frank will struggle as best he can even though he knows it is useless. One grabs him by the hair and forces his head back, and when he is finally pinned down the doctor and his assistant arrive.

Various methods will be employed to open Frank's mouth: his nose will be covered to cut off air, or a screw or doctor will bunch his fists and bore his knuckles into the joints on each side of the jaws. A Ryle's tube will be used. This is a very long, thin tube which is pushed through the nose. It is supposedly for nasal feeding but, in force-feeding, it is simply a weapon used to force open the jaws. It rubs against the membrane at the back of the nose and, if not coated in lubricant (it seldom is), it causes a searing pain, akin to a red-hot needle being pushed into one's head. If Frank cries out, a wooden clamp will immediately be pushed between his teeth. If this fails to work the doctor will use a large pair of forceps to cut into the gums, the ensuing pain again forcing the jaws to open sufficiently for the clamp to be pressed in. Sometimes a metal clamp, rather liked a "bulldog" clip, is used. It is shoved between the teeth and a bolt is turned, opening a spring and forcing the jaws apart.

When Frank's jaws are finally prised open a wooden bit, rather like a horse's bit, is forced into his mouth. It "sits" across his mouth with a screw holding each end, and there is a hole in the centre of it through which the feeding tube passes. A flat piece of wood is used to press the tongue down and then a three-foot-long rubber tube, coated in liquid paraffin, is shoved in and down his throat. A funnel is placed on the open end and some water poured in. If the water bubbles they know the tube is in Frank's lungs. If so, the tube is removed and the process starts again. Michael Gaughan was murdered in this way. When the tube is eventually fixed properly it is pushed down into Frank's stomach.

There are different widths of tube and obviously the wider they are the more painful the torture. Doctors usually use the widest as it gets the food down quicker and they don't have to delay overlong. Frank will feel his stomach filling up and stretching, an experience he has undergone before. Automatically he will vomit, the disgorged food being caught in a kidney-dish. If the doctor in charge is especially sadistic the vomit will be forced back down his throat again (as happened to Gerry Kelly). When the tube is being removed it tears at the back of the throat, more so than before because the liquid paraffin will have worn off on the way down. The last few inches will be ghastly. Frank will get violent pains in his chest. He will choke and, at this point, he will be sicker than before, as the tube coming out triggers off more retching (Marion Price passed out at this stage once). After "feeding" Frank will find it impossible to stand up, to sit up, or to move in any way.

Frank Stagg is also on thirst strike. This is dealt with in two ways. The first method employed is simply more force-feeding with fluids in the food. Since this liquid by-passes his mouth (via the tube) that is where he will feel it most. The other method involves putting extra salt in the liquid during force-feeding. This causes a more concentrated dehydration and increases the desire for water. To alternate repeatedly between thirst and hunger strike, as Frank is doing, is extremely difficult and inde-scribably agonizing. He may be refused a towel or water to wash off his vomit, as Hugh Feeney was, and his cell will stink of sour milk and disgorged food. On one occasion Hugh Feeney was denied Communion by a priest, so Frank could find himself denied even spiritual comfort.

This, then, is a basic description of the barbarism condoned by English politicians in England and con-demned by them elsewhere. It is inflicted with equal savagery on women as on men. Dolours and Marion Price were tortured like this during a strike which lasted 205 days. But what of conditions for other Republican POWs and for Frank Stagg if he were not on hunger strike? These conditions can be divided into two cate-gories: the conditions within the ordinary association system, and conditions under solitary confinement.

Frank Stagg, even if he were not on hunger strike, would be held in solitary confinement as punishment for his refusal to do labour or wear prison clothes. He is held under Rule 43 G.O.D (Good Order and Discipline) which is a type of internment within the ordinary gaol system, inasmuch as it overrides even the most perfunctory gaol charges and sentences, usually passed by the prison Board of Visitors in "normal" circumstances. Under Rule 43 the prisoner need not face any charge and he can be kept in solitary confinement indefinitely, under any pretext, on orders from the Governor. Segregation blocks vary but the procedure adopted is more or less the same throughout all the prisons in England. It is at present being used against nearly all Republican POWs. Under the solitary confinement rule they are allowed no contact or communication with other prisoners. They are forbidden to speak to anyone. Screws are instructed not to converse with POWs and should a POW try to communicate with anyone extra "disciplinary measures" are ordered. The cell is bare during the day, with bedding, mattress and, if possible, the bed itself being removed at seven o'clock each morning. The red night-light is replaced with an extra-bright fluorescent one. Always the cell is lit up, making sleep impossible. Because Frank has refused to wear prison clothes, he is naked, but he is allowed one threadbare grey blanket which can be taken from him at a minute's notice without explanation: it is a privilege! His shoulders, elbows, knees and hips chafe from the friction of the blanket and the concrete surface of the cell. This has a similiar effect to a severe dose of sunburn. There is no heating in the cells, which are bare, always damp, cold and very, very dirty.

In such a cell Frank Stagg and his comrades will be found, sitting or lying, always on the floor and always, always in a corner. This posture is a commonsense one because here he will avoid, to a degree, the draughts which sweep the cells. He always attempts, in vain, to cover himself completely with his blanket (if he is lucky or privileged enough to have one). At half past seven he will be given a basin of hot water in which he washes himself. Immediately this is done, the basin is removed. The hot water would have allowed him to warm his feet and that is not allowed. He is then permitted to "slop out". His breakfast is left in and at about 10.30 the Governor and Doctor make their rounds. Both will stand in the doorway, look, nod, comment on the weather and leave. His health will never be mentioned while he continues to breathe. Prison staff may goad and attempt to annoy the POW. At 11.30 the breakfast is removed and the dinner is left in. At 4.30 the dinner is removed and the tea is left in. The cell is searched every day. A bare, empty dungeon with a naked man in one corner, but it is searched anyway and a screw checks it at least once every half-hour.

An internal body search may be ordered. The POW will be forced to touch his toes and a screw, wearing plastic gloves, will probe and search his rear passage. At eight o'clock the bedding is returned and at nine the white fluorescent light is replaced again by the red one. All night the screw checks the cell at least twice an hour. Sleep is impossible. The cell reeks from the smell of stale food. The POW spends his time trying to keep warm and always he fails. Frank Stagg is not allowed to leave his cell and he has existed like this, as have most Republican POWs, for two years. Exercise facilities, for those lucky enough to get them, vary from goal to goal, but usually they are conducted once a day in a cage seven paces by nine paces. Half an hour is the allotted time, if the weather permits, and the elements, like everything else, are controlled by the Governor who refuses exercise periods as he pleases.

Republican POWs, on account of their refusal to work, have to depend on one free letter a week and they will be cheerfully informed by screws of letters being stopped, of letters submitted to the Home Office and of their own out-going mail being held by the prison authorities because the POW dared to mention conditions.

Visits operate around two main principles. POWs get visits in a closed room, as opposed to the communal visiting room. A governor and screw sit within three feet, taking notes of conversations, regardless of how intimate they are, between the POW and his visitor. Physical contact with loved ones, the embracing of husband and wife, children and parents, is strictly forbidden. If the POW or his visitor try to whisper, or if voices drop at all, the visit is stopped.

The other visits fall into the "closed" category. That is, the POW and his visitor are separated from each other and conversations (under the same conditions as above) are conducted through a grille. Screws are always present, one behind the POW watching his visitor, the other behind the visitor, watching the POW. The governor sits in to record the conversation.

These are the conditions which relatives have to endure after travelling from Ireland to see their loved ones. Roy Walsh, at the minute in solitary in Wormwood Scrubs, in the segregation unit there, is separated from his comrades with whom he had protested in November last year. He and they will find themselves on numerous charges as punishment for their courageous protest. For each charge these three POWs can be given fifty-six days solitary with loss of all privileges. All the sentences can run consecutively and during this period the number of visits will be cut in half, as will the time of the visit itself. In 1974 a prisoner called Stephen Smith died in the Segregation Unit; the open verdict returned at his inquest speaks for itself.

As far as "conditions under the ordinary prison system" are concerned, even those POWs allowed into the wings have no respite from the very discriminate persecution by the prison administration. It is carried out in every possible way. Out-going and incoming mail is stopped or "mislaid". Educational and gym facilities, open to other prisoners, are refused to the POW. Visits are conducted as described above and this persecution can be and is spread to take in prisoners who associate with the POWs. This, indeed, is an accepted way to alienate Republican POWs from other prisoners, and screws constantly do their utmost to aggravate the situation and to create confrontations between the POWs and the other prisoners. The fight between the Republican POWs and the prison authorities is continuous and the POWs are forever under pressure from the administration. Conditions are similar to those imposed on POWs in Ireland, in gaols north and south of the Border. But in Ireland at least the prisoners have the company of comrades and their close-ness to home to sustain them. In England the prisoners are tortured and all possible pressure is exerted to break and isolate them. Despite this, the Irish Ambassador to Britain, unlike his British counterpart to Chile, remains at his post in London and the Dublin government's only concern is of a Quisling nature. In Portlaoise, the "Joy" and Limerick gaols, they match British brutality, torture to torture.

Lack of space and difficulties in communication restrict this account of conditions in English jails. I have mentioned some names as they came up but many, many more have been left out. Frank Stagg and the POWs in England fight against a system which has not changed since Ó Donnabháin Rossa was shackled hand and foot in 1870, when Irish prisoners were driven to insanity. Conditions have not changed since Toirlach Mac Suibhne died in Brixton Prison.

The London government is at war with the IRA. This was re-declared in 1971 by Reginald Maudling. The POWs are in England because of this war and POWs, as Airey Neave discovered even in Colditz, have rights. They have rights and these rights must be upheld as the rights of Dr Sheila Cassidy in Chile should be upheld. The English government will never afford any rights to imprisoned Irish men and women unless they are forced to do so.

The Dublin government has abandoned its responsibility to its own citizens. It actively undermines their rights. Only the Irish people can guarantee these rights. They can do this by opposing the British presence in Ireland and the injustices and torture meted out to Irish prisoners.

Frank Stagg died on 12 February, 1976.

THE CHANGE WILL DO US GOOD

Your Man has been growing onions (a moderate variety which he calls his Conor Cruise O'Briens) and shamrock (which he just calls shamrock). He grows them, separately of course, in jam jars. The shamrock has been struggling since St Patrick's Day and Your Man has had to liberate it a few times from the screws. They steal it on raids. Long Kesh, Your Man says, is no place for the Green. He is his usual self but Cedric has been much more aggressive lately and Egbert has been in a big D for ages now. He and Cedric have even stopped debating. They just lie in the sun and, with the recent warm weather, we have seen celibate republican bone structures which haven't been naked in years.

Your Man is also breeding ladybirds and caterpillars. One of his caterpillars turned into a butterfly the other night. He was up all night preventing everyone else from going to sleep as he muttered about the absence of hot water, the difficulty of birth and the lack of proper post-natal facilities. He says his new offspring is a girl. How he can tell no one knows, but we suspect his too many long years in here are catching up on him. I must say, however, that she is very beautiful. Brown and orange and red in

125

colour. We call her Irma la Douce. It's nice to have a female about the place, even if she is only a baby butterfly.

We got moved once again on Monday. That makes it the third shift this year. It's all part of the prison regime's anti-escape strategy. The screws caught our tunnel and they got excited and decided that we should be moved, even though it was only a wee tunnel (despite being started months ago) and we only had the shaft finished. And because we had nowhere else to live, after the way the Brits' raiding party messed up the huts, we set off for Cage Four. Since then, comrades, things have improved considerably. A change, as Your Man says, is as good as a rest.

Perhaps I should explain about Cage Four. If you're driving down the M1 towards Belfast, Cage Four is on the left beside the second Brit post on the perimeter wall. You can't miss it. Cage Four sits a wee bit back from the wall almost at right angles to Cage Five, which is parallel and closer to the perimeter wall. Cage Eleven is miles away in the middle of the camp and Cage Four, up at the perimeter, is in the internees' end.

Anyway, Cage Four has cheered me up a wee bit. For one thing there's loads of grass outside the cage, close to the wire, and great clumps of it inside, in the yard. Then there are wee corners where a fella can get a bit of quiet and a good gaze at the no-man's-land between us and the perimeter. Buttercups, jaggy nettles, thistles and pooley-the-beds are thriving on Brit weedkiller and although most of the no-man's-land is plucked clean of cover and colour, the hardy weeds nearest the cage fencing are most cheerful. Cedric reckons the smells are fantastic and, as we have just moved up-wind from the burnhouse, nobody is arguing with him.

Then, of course, there is the M1. We can see it from the roof of our huts. "Thon's a bus, a wee car and a tipper lorry," Egbert announced excitedly the first time he got up. At that we all scrambled on the roof and looked out at Hillsborough church steeple, at the monument behind it, at the wee fields and, of course, at the motorway itself. Cedric was the first one to spot the cows, or cattle as he called them, but Egbert trumped him by drawing our attention to the trees, the whitewashed church to their right and the woman putting her washing out on a hedge about ten fields away. Plus, as he screamed, "the radio mast at Hillsborough aroundabout that you pass going to Dublin".

And then there's the wildlife. In our old cage, not counting our pigeons which aren't really wildlife, we had only a few starlings, seagulls, screws, the odd mouse, loads of crows and an epidemic of sparrows. I almost forgot about the hawks. For as long as I've been in Long Kesh a pair of hawks have hunted here. They dine well on the wee birds and other livestock. But they don't always get things their own way: sometimes squadrons of sparrows gather like a huge black cloud to chase them off. As we lie here on our backs watching the perfectly choreographed aerial dogfights, Your Man, as always the romantic, asks, "D'y'know what that proves? That proves unity is strength. On their own them sparrows have no chance but together – just look at them." And we do, enthralled at the flawlessly synchronised formations of the life and death battles acted out with deadly intent far above us in the azure-blue sky. Cynical Cedric, he of the smart-alec answer, remarks that Your Man never seems to contemplate what would happen if all the hawks got together.

The sight of a hawk has always filled me with awe: perhaps because they are so individualistic; because they are hunting and I wonder what and where is their prey; or perhaps because I know I'm afraid of them. One of the country lads here calls them murderers; not because they kill, but because they kill other birds. He's deadly serious, too.

We usually know when they're about because all the small birds get excited. They cut for cover so that after the first brief fluttering panic the sky is suddenly deserted except for the one or two ominous dots high above, like twin Skibbereen eagles keeping an eye on us all.

A few months ago we watched as one of them dropped like a stone to swoop on a small bird on the tarmacked gap between Cages Six and Twenty-Two. We applauded and yahooed when the hawk, rising again with its victim clutched in its claws, flew headlong into the wire. For a second or two it lay stunned on the ground while its dinner skedaddled at speed.

I haven't seen a hawk up at this end of the camp, at least not yet. All seems peaceful and from the corner of this cage, the corner nearest the perimeter, a few pleasant hours can be passed day-dreaming and birdwatching. Grey hooded crows drift in and out of the camp at ease; finches are plentiful; twice we've seen magpies, and racing-pigeons from some nearby loft circle overhead each evening, dipping in and sweeping out again in formation. Starlings feed their delinquent younkers on POW breadcrumbs, but favourite of all are the larks. At least, Cedric says they're larks. Egbert swears that they're swifts and Your Man only withdrew his suggestion about swallows when they both pounced on him. I reckon they're larks myself and each day we have spied them climb high into the sky, their shrill piping sounding above the swoosh of the motorway traffic, and watched amazed and envious as they glided effortlessly to their nests outside the perimeter. In Long Kesh the humans look out of their cages at the birds or, as Your Man remarked, the birds look into the cages at the people.

On Tuesday we discovered a cat with three little kittens living among the weeds under an old chair, and since then a captive audience has watched anxiously for Brit war-dogs while mother cat has fed, cleaned or played with her kittens. The camp is breeding a pretty substantial family of semi-wild cats since a lonely internee first introduced a tiny tom-kitten to life behind the wire in late '71. There was a plague of mice which conquered all for some years until the cats multiplied and culled the wee mouses. Now the cats live well in our barbed-wire wilderness, coming into the cages for food and slipping out at night to sleep on the other side of the cage fencing.

One black-and-white kitten in the Cage Four family has a cut eye which has turned septic, but we can only look sympathetically at him as he stumbles clumsily after his more lively brother and sister. He probably won't survive the winter.

Opposite where I'm sitting, bored brits with ragged-tailed alsatians patrol the perimeter ceaselessly. They trudge past us, up by Cage Five, around by the football pitch beside Cage Three, down alongside Cage Seven and back up again from Cage Eight. The new walls separate us from the cell-blocks which sprawl towards the motorway, preventing us from following the lark's flight as it teases us with its ability to leave the camp while we humans, the supposedly superior beings, are forced to remain stranded on the ground. POWs' cat and kittens, cheeky-headed sparrows and the ever-mocking larks gaze at screws and Brits as they patrol their eternal beats. Cage Four isn't really much different from Cage Eleven, but the change will do us no harm and, in our typical Long Kesh fashion, we will miss it when we are moved back to the reconstructed scene of our erstwhile tunnel.

Then we will recall the *craic* we had, the escape which would have worked if we had been left a wee bit longer, and the way the M1 glistened and swayed in the sticky sunshine. Some will recall that it was in Cage Five on a Sunday in June, while the rest of the internees in the cage were assembling for their weekly parade, that Paddy Crawford died a death of quiet desperation. He slipped into the one of the huts and hanged himself. Others may recall that Hugh Coney was killed within a hundred yards of the lark's nest and that Paddy Teer died in Cage Four before it housed remand prisoners. That the M1, the birds, the cats, even the sun can't be seen from the new cell-blocks and that Republican prisoners will be in there before winter, when the scabby-eyed kitten will be no more, and even the ladybirds will have deserted the few surviving jaggy nettles. We will still be here, of course; more comfortable than the prisoners in England, happier than the lads in the Crum, the women in Armagh or the men in the cell-blocks. Stormont, depending on the ability of the IRA and the agility of the SDLP, may or may not have returned and the British troops, Ulsterised or Anglified, will still patrol catwalks in concentration camps and back-streets or country roads in that greater prison outside.

Egbert says that Britain doesn't really want to stay here, and that the British government would actually be glad to be rid of us. That's why he and Cedric stopped debating. Cedric insists that when England declares her lack of interest in public and starts making rapid arrangements to withdraw that will be soon enough to begin to believe it. Your Man agrees with Cedric of course. He says that until then, "Blandly asserted convictions with no substance to support them" must remain suspect!

In the meantime, we do our whack in the sun, this side of the M1, just behind the second Brit post on your left as you speed towards Belfast. You can't miss it, even if you're driving too fast to see the lark or to hear him slagging us. There will always be someone here while the Brit remains and, as Your Man says, "The Brit will always be here until he is forced to leave". Even then he will only leave with reluctance. But then that change, I have no doubt, will do us good. It will be even better than a rest.

THE NIGHT ANDY WARHOL WAS BANNED

The Camp OC isn't a bad sort. In fact, in his own way, he is a decent spud. He is older than the rest of us. I suppose you could say he is from the older school of Belfast Republicans. There is a fairly large number of them in with us, including a few old-age pensioners, and between them I suppose they have served a thousand-odd years of imprisonment. The way they talk about the thirties, the forties and the fifties, that's the way it sounds. Before many of us were born they had a few years of heavy whack behind them.

I'm not joking either when I say they served a thousand years, a lot of it without charge or trial. In fact, they may have served longer. Say there are between about ninety and 120 of them spread throughout the camp. Say they served an average of five years in the fifties and another five years in the forties, plus this stretch. Then count the few dozen who did a bit of time in the thirties, plus Liam Mulholland who was first imprisoned in 1919 (they say he and Wolfe Tone were cell-mates, though I wouldn't believe that), and add it all up and you get a few centuries of porridge. Anyway, that's why you have to be a bit tolerant of them. They've learned that all things come to pass so they do their whack gracefully and with a certain grey-haired dignity. Most of the time. Other times they take up principled positions over things we young ones don't even understand. Then they throw us and the prison regime into a crisis.

Other times they get uptight about more mundane matters. For example, there are times when they refuse to eat the prison grub. Well, you may think, that's up to them! But, on account of the Camp OC being one of their contemporaries, an injury to one becomes an injury to all and we, upon the OC's instructions to the screws to take away the food – we all starve. It isn't too bad if some of our clique have a food parcel but, as Cedric noted, usually they refuse the grub when they have *their* food parcels.

Most of our senior citizens are in Cage Twenty-Two, an internment cage for geriatric delinquent subversives like our Camp OC. But, as Your Man says, being there, or here, doesn't necessarily make you a bad person. In fact, in his own way the Camp OC is a decent enough spud. Except on the issue of sex. He has strange ideas about sex. I suppose at his age you couldn't expect anything else. That's why he banned Andy Warhol. Well, he didn't actually ban Andy in person; his authority isn't quite as extensive as that. What I mean is that he banned us from watching Andy Warhol a few weeks ago on BBC2.

It was Cedric who put us on to it. He was reading the TV page. "Listen to this, lads: explicit sexual scenes in programme about Andy Warhol."

At around the same time one of the younger old men in Cage Twenty-Two was reading the same article. He put his feet, both of them, right in it. "Explicit sexual scenes," he leered hopefully. That was enough. One of the more decrepit comrades heard him and went off, like a right oul' sloppy tit, and told the Camp OC. It was after that we got the word: "All POWs are banned from watching the television programme about Andy Warhol".

Funny enough, everyone took the news quietly and calmly. Of course, Your Man reared up and when none of us would agree to join him in protest he turned his anger against me and Cedric and Egbert. Machiavelli, he isn't. We ignored him. Over in Cage Twenty-Two we heard that a terrible noration was being raised by the comrade who had first read of the offending programme. He became quite obstreperous.

"The struggle is about freedom," he protested, "about freedom of expression, an end to censorship. You can't ban TV programmes."

The Camp OC was unmoved. Some Republicans are like that. If he had been a rocking horse the OC wouldn't even have given a nod.

"I've sent the same directive all around this camp. Over a thousand men have received it and no one has complained. I expect more from you. You should be giving a better example to the younger men."

And right too. He had sent his directive all round the camp. Over a thousand of us did receive it and not one of us complained. The programme was broadcast on a Wednesday night. Cage Twenty-Two was the only one which didn't see it.

They didn't miss much. And we didn't enlighten them. You see, we wouldn't offend our Camp OC for the world. He isn't a bad old spud. And what he doesn't know will do him no harm.

IN DEFENCE OF DANNY LENNON

On 10 August 1976 three young people died in Belfast. Two were young children, the other a young man. Later a third child died, and with his death a young family was almost wiped out. The Maguire family, understandably enough, have condemned the IRA and Mr Maguire, whose wife still remains seriously ill in hospital, has been forthright in his condemnation of the republican movement.

I accept his feelings and I can understand that he feels every justification for saying what he did. He has lost his children and no words of mine, nor of anyone else, can hope to encompass the loss which is his. All I can do is to offer my condolences to the Maguire family. If they refuse to accept this, I will understand. If I am condemned as a hypocrite, I will understand. I know there is nothing I can do to break down the feeling of animosity which the families bereaved in the past few years may hold towards those they feel are responsible for their loss.

This letter may be misrepresented or misunderstood by many people, as republicanism itself has been misunderstood and misrepresented by many people. There can be no defence against that. Readers have the right to form their own opinions about my sincerity and about the sincerity of the republican movement.

I do not write on my own behalf and I have no authority to speak for the movement. I, on a personal level, and the movement itself as an organization must bear the responsibility and must face any criticism in the knowledge that we are not always in the best position to justify our stand, our philosophy and our activities.

We can and we must do our utmost to ensure that everything we do will have the minimum effect on those people with no vested interest in opposing us and we must, on a personal level, ensure that our conduct, our discipline and our attitude will encourage, not discourage continued support for the republican cause.

This letter, then, is to those people who have no vested interest in opposing us. I do not seek to change opinions about myself, about republicanism, about violence, about the IRA nor the republican leadership. Think what you will, good or bad about these, I, from Long Kesh, can do little to influence you. Only those Republicans on the outside, by their actions, attitudes and conduct, can do that.

I intend speaking here for the young man who was killed. I am deeply sorry that three young children died. I know that he would feel the same and that he would have done everything in his power to prevent injury or death to those innocent of any responsibility for the situation in which the Irish people now find themselves. Children are always innocent. The Maguire family were not Danny Lennon's enemies and he was not their enemy. They were victims of circumstances created when he was shot dead.

He did not point a weapon at them. He did not drive the car at them. He was dead before the car crashed. That much was conceded by the British Army.

Danny Lennon went out with a weapon against the people he had identified as enemies. He went out against the British Army and he knew the risks he was taking. He did not willingly involve others in that risk and his death, which came as a consequence of his actions, is all the more tragic because a young family died with him. He meant no harm to anyone other than the people who eventually killed him; and even then it was the system they represented which he was opposed to.

Danny Lennon became involved in the republican movement in August 1971. He came into jail in October 1972 and he was released on 30 April 1976. He did not have to go back to the IRA. Three-and-a-half years in Long Kesh and his time on the run before that left him with no illusions about how hard the struggle for national freedom is nor how easy it is to become confused and demoralised. He knew what he was fighting for and was articulate in speaking about the kind of Ireland that the Irish people could make their own.

He wasn't a young man caught up in violence. Second-timers (those who have been in and out of jail) know what it's about. Danny Lennon cared nothing for myths, for personalities, for glory-hunting. He sidestepped the petty material things which could have been his. He believed in a society where exploitation of people by people would cease. He recognized the sacrifices needed to secure this and he died in circumstances which he had dedicated his life to preventing.

His death, which robbed the Maguire children of their lives, was a contradiction of a life spent fighting for young children such as they.

Danny Lennon recognized that force, with all its hardships and tragedy, can be justified only by those who know what they are fighting for and by those willing to fight, by those willing to share the hardship. He spent his last few months in this cage reading Pearse and Connolly, updating in his own fashion the threads of our republican philosophy.

He knew what was right and what was wrong. He was a human being, a young man of twenty-three with a mother and father, brothers and sisters. He had human feelings and weaknesses like the rest of us. Like us all he made mistakes but he was a good young man, a socialist by instinct and an IRA operator by choice. He wanted an Ireland free of the profit-motive, free of fighting, free from sectarianism and free from violence. He did not fight for some outdated ideal, for some abstract thing: he fought for a society in which the Irish people could be truly a sovereign people.

You may not accept this. You may believe that violence is never justified. You may have suffered; you may not want any trouble. You may be weary, sick, old or tired. I do not seek to change your attitudes, to rob you of your opinions. I only ask that you accept that the Danny Lennons within the republican movement would, if given the chance, help to build a society in Ireland worthy of the men, women and children of Ireland and that they are engaged in the struggle for this without thought of personal gain or recognition.

To the Maguire family and to the Lennon family I offer my sincere condolences. If I am misunderstood by those who have a vested interest, a political interest, in misconstruing this letter, I accept the consequences. If it is used to attack me or the republican movement, so be it. If for one minute it allows readers to understand the many Danny Lennons who have been attacked and denounced by people older, greedier and more mercenary than themselves, his struggle will not have been in vain.

For all the dead who died for Ireland and for all the dead who died in Ireland, Jesus have pity. None of us stands guiltless; only our children are innocent. It remains for us to ensure that we build a society in which they will not be robbed of their innocence. Then and only then will we have the peace that ordinary people everywhere deserve and desire.

ONLY JOKING

"Big Domnic O'Filibuster was the best mixer I ever met," Your Man was adamant.

"Nawh," Cedric snorted scornfully. "He was only a wee boy compared to Dipper Dedalus."

"What are you arguing about?" asked Egbert.

"About who was the best at stirring things up, putting in the mix, before we all settled down to do our whack," I explained.

"Awh that's easy. Domnic!" Egbert replied knowledgeably.

"Listen to him," Cedric almost screamed. "He'd rather be wrong than be quiet. He's only here a meal hour. How would you know who was the best mixer?" he accused Egbert.

"Well," Egbert replied quietly and with a finesse that both Domnic and Dipper would have envied, "it's easier to be objective if you're not involved. Yours is a subjective recollection, probably biased by your closeness to the situation. I'm uninvolved and therefore impartial and objective, and Domnic gets my vote."

"Domnic's not looking for your vote. You're not even in this conversation!"

"Hold on, Cedric," Your Man pleaded, "Egbert's got a point."

"My arse!" Cedric spluttered. "He's winding me up. He knows nothing about big Domnic or Dipper."

"Is that so?" Egbert asked smugly. "Remember the time Domnic asked the new screw to get him a bap and the *Irish News*?"

"Aye," Your Man's face lit up at the memory. "He went out to the gate about half-eight one morning, gave the new screw a ten-bob note and asked him to run down to the shop for ten Park Drive, a bap and the *Irish News*."

"I remember that," Cedric conceded warmly. "That was quare *craic*. Especially when the screw came back half an hour later and returned the ten-bob note."

"He said he couldn't find the shop," Egbert chortled.

"And 'member he asked the Gov'nor for a piano?" Cedric continued. "The negotiations went on for weeks. It was an English gov'nor and he hadn't much sense. Domnic really wound him up."

"Just proves my point," said Egbert.

"Wha'?"

"I'm just saying that you're proving my point," Egbert repeated softly.

"No way. I, I never said Domnic wasn't a good mixer. I only said he wasn't as good as Dipper."

"What about big Mick?" Your Man asked.

"Now there was a man who was born with a wooden spoon," Cedric was glad of a reprieve. "He never stopped stirring. Remember he set up a mousetrap in Cage Six? He fixed electric wires to a steel tray, then plugged it in and set it just beside the hut toilet."

"Was he trying to catch the mice doing a piddle?"

"No, he was trying to catch us doing a piddle. No laughing matter when you're dying for a piss in the middle of the night, in the dark. 'If you splash, you flash,' big Mick used to shout from his bunk."

"A really crazy man," Egbert volunteered. "He used to walk around the yard, stark naked, pretending he was walking a dog. He had a piece of cable, almost rigid it was, which he fashioned into a dog lead and he walked around with an invisible dog on the end of it. The new men never knew what to make of him. We used to set them up: 'Never mind big Mick,' we'd say."

"What about the escapes?" I asked.

"Aye, they were great – big Domnic's speciality," Egbert reminded us.

"There was more than big Domnic set men up for escapes," Cedric retaliated. "Dipper was great at that. Most new men fell for it; we would ask them to create a diversion," he explained to me, "and of course there would be no escape at all. It was quare *craic*. Men fainting in front of screws; or keeping watch with their faces blackened, ready to sing out if they heard a noise. Of course, we always arranged that for them. Then as they raised the alarm by singing we'd switch on the lights. Ha, ha, ha, I can still see their wee black faces as the whole hut erupted laughing and they realized they were set up."

"Aye," Egbert agreed, excited at the memory, "and the water fights and putting bread on the roof of another hut so that the seagulls came down for breakfast and wakened everyone."

"That was banned quickly here," Your Man recalled. "It caused awful rows. Scores of seagulls pecking and fighting on the tin roof at dawn isn't very comradely."

"What about Domnic getting the new men to go to the gate with their towels waiting for a bus to take them out for a swim," Egbert returned to his theme. "Dipper never did anything as good as that. They used to stand there in a queue!" he roared at the memory.

"And there was a young fella called Dusty used to make a lot of noise in bed every night. And then Domnic painted a big eye on Dusty's bed-sheets with the words *We're watching you* below it. Dusty was furious. He changed his sheets around, and on the other side there was a big ear with *And we're listening to you as well*! I thought he'd explode when he saw it," Egbert burst out. "Still, it soon quietened him down at night, I must say."

"I was talking about Dipper," Cedric started valiantly.

Egbert ignored him. "What about the confessions? I've great stories to tell about confessions. When new lads came in on remand we'd tell them the priest was in and if they wanted to go to confession he'd be in the study hut. Well, we told them that, with very serious parental faces on us, and of course it nearly always worked. Off they'd go to the study hut, but instead of a priest inside . . ."

"Would be big Domnic," Cedric mimicked. "Everybody knows this yarn. He'd have a blanket up and half the men in the cage behind it and the other half hanging off the hut like blue-bottles around . . ."

"Sshhh," Your Man interrupted. "Let Egbert tell it. It's his story."

"It's everybody's story!" Cedric protested.

"Well I started it so I'll finish it," retorted Egbert.

"It'll be the first thing you ever finished."

"Domnic," Egbert repeated slowly as he glared across at Cedric, "Domnic would be behind a blanket draped across the hut and he'd have a boxing glove on. You get the picture? He'd begin the confession just as any priest and he'd start to ease all the lad's sins out of him and then, when the lad admitted some particular offence, he'd shout: 'You did what?' and he'd whack out with the boxing glove! It was really something to see. An arm with the boxing glove on the end of it coming round the edge of the blanket. The young lad staring at it in disbelief, then wham!

"And you, ha, ha, you know, nobody ever looked behind the blanket. Even when they got whacked a few times. They just went on with their confession. Ha, ha, ha. One young lad ended up cowering in his seat in dread of the boxing glove as he made a clean breast of things."

"What kind of sins did they confess?" Your Man asked with interest.

"Oh nothing much. I mean, no mortal sins; all venial ones. Only telling lies, losing their tempers, masturbating – that was worth two punches. Ha, ha, ha. Oh, big

Domnic was a geg. I remember another time . . ."

"I remember a time too," Cedric shouted, grimly determined to have his say. "I remember a time when some of us worked a double-mix around confessions. There was a guy in our cage when we were on remand and he'd do the confessions and he'd always wind the new wee lads up, asking them had they got a girl and did they ever drop the hand."

"That's bad talk," Egbert put in. "Trust you. You bust in here mouthing off about Dipper and then you start to bring sex into it. It's not on."

"Hang on, hang on," Cedric huffed with indignation. "Let me finish."

"Aye, let him finish," Your Man agreed.

"Well, one day we got a new lad and then we set up our friend." He paused; "We'll call him Bloggs. We set him up as nice as could be. Bloggs did the confession business as usual and we were in behind the blanket with him and the new lad was out in front.

"'Well, son,' said Bloggs, 'have you a girlfriend?'

"'I have, Father, and I'm afraid I'm in a bit of trouble.'

"Bloggs nearly burst. He had a job keeping back his laughter. 'He's in trouble,' he whispered to us behind the blanket and then barely containing himself he asked,

"'What kind of trouble, my son?'

"'She's pregnant, Father.'

"By now," Cedric continued, "Bloggs was nearly beside himself. He had half his pullover shoved in his mouth and every other second he'd nudge us. He was delighted.

"'Would you like me to visit the girl?' he asked.

"'Father, I'd be very obliged if you would. She lives in Andersonstown.'

"'That's where I live,' Bloggs whispered to us between mouthfulls of pullover as his face grew redder and redder and the tears started down his face with the effort not to laugh out loud.

"'Whereabouts in Andersonstown, my son?'

"'In Andersonstown Terrace, Father.'

"'Awh,' Bloggs wheezed at us from the floor, tears tripping him up and the giggles starting to burst through. 'That's my street. What a cracker!'

"'And what is the girl's name?' he asked eventually.

"'Bloggs, Father. You might know her Da.'

"Gee whizz," Egbert whistled in admiration as the rest of us burst into applause. "That's a great mix. What happened?"

"There was holy murder. Bloggs went through the blanket at the wee lad. He never, ever forgave him. And he had to get a special visit before he'd believe it was a mix."

"Like the time the Brits came in and challenged Ed to a fair dig," Egbert offered. "When he refrained they got very annoyed, calling him a welcher, and then they beat him up. Ed was shattered. He didn't mind being beat up, but his pride? He used to be proud when he was young. His pride was hurt at being called a welcher. Later we discovered it was Todler's fault. Unbeknownst to Ed he had pinned a notice on the bottom of Ed's bed, warning that big Ed was a lean, mean, fighting machine. It suggested he ate Brits. Poor Ed wouldn't hurt a fly. The Brits weren't a bit pleased. Nor was poor Ed. Ed was very annoyed at Todler for that, so he was."

"That's like you taking the needle when the legs of your jeans were sewed up the morning there was a British Army raid," Cedric chuckled.

"I didn't take the needle," Egbert contradicted him. "I was just a wee bit upset. It wasn't fair, making an eejit of me in front of the Brits. Not a very republican thing to do.

"And it wasn't really having my jeans sewn up that annoyed me. When I tripped getting them on I twigged to what was wrong. It was when I got another pair out of my locker and they were sewed up as well and then the sleeves of my jacket too! I never did find out who did it. I got three days solitary for hitting a Brit who laughed at me. That wasn't funny."

We all laughed. "You were always too angry for

anyone to admit it," Cedric told him. "Anyway, now that you seem to be over it, I'd be delighted to tell you."

The rest of us waited in anticipation as he paused at the door of the hut.

"Do you want to know, Egbert?" he teased.

"Cedric, I don't really care if I never know. There's mixing and mixing and that was out of order, but I wouldn't like to fall out with anyone now about it so don't tell me."

"OK, old friend," Cedric agreed as he slammed the door behind him. A second later the door re-opened and he poked his head in again. "Who did you say was the best mixer?"

"Domnic," Egbert replied without hesitation.

"You're right."

"What?"

"You're right!"

"I thought you said Dipper was the best."

"I did, but Dipper never sewed up all your clothes. That was a classic. That was Domnic."

The door slammed closed again.

"You know," said Egbert in disgust, as he looked around at our laughing faces, "there are smart-alecs all around Ireland and the British government chooses to put most of them in this cage and me with youse. Just remember," he snapped, "remember! He who laughs last, laughs last. I'll get my own back on the lot of youse!"

DEAR JOHN

"What!" I exclaimed.

Your Man sighed sadly. He leaned back in his chair until it was tilted on two legs with its back resting against the wall of the study hut. He eased his legs out from under the table and balanced himself with his feet on the table-top. He stared at the ceiling, then, swallowing hard and averting his gaze from mine, he replied, "Sinead has left me. She's taking the kids to live in England."

"When did you find this out?"

"Today. On the visit. Well, I found out for definite today. She talked about it before; we both did. Remember last year? When I told you she wasn't coming up because she was sick? Well, she wasn't sick. She was just browned off with the searches and the British Army outside the camp, the screws on the visit, and all the messing about getting ready and the annoyance with the kids. And then before we'd know it the half-hour would be up and it was time to start waiting for the next half-hour – the following week."

Your Man's tone was despondently even. He continued to stare at the ceiling.

"To make matters worse we don't . . . " he corrected himself, "we didn't live in a republican area. So she used to come up on her own in her brother's car. You know the way all our people come up on the bus, well most of them do, and they get a bit of *craic* and, you know, it all helps. Sinead always felt a bit of an outsider."

"You should have said. Sure there's plenty of our people to give a wee bit of support," I protested. "She could have – she could still go out with Colette and Anne-Marie and all that crowd. Why don't you arrange for . . ."

"Nawh, mucker, it's too late," he interrupted me. "And don't be annoying yourself. I suggested all that. I even got my sisters to take her out. Nawh, it isn't that. Sinead just never got married for this. She got married to be married. It's not her fault. It's a wonder she stuck it so long – it's three years now. Our Sean's five and wee Mairead's nearly four. Not much of a life for any of them, is it?"

He swung his legs down off the table and hunched forward in his chair. He stared blankly at the study-hut door. I could see the tears welling up in his eyes.

"I'm going to miss the kids," he declared eventually, sucking in his cheeks and blowing out a long, deep breath. "That's why Sinead didn't go before this. She knew I loved the kids up on a visit."

"Maybe it's a phase she's going through. Once it's out of her system she'll be all right," I offered.

"Nawh," Your Man smiled wryly at me, "this is no phase. This is for keeps. Sinead's a realist. I've another nine years to do, you know. That's not much of a future. So we decided that we'd separate."

"You agreed!" I exclaimed.

"Aye," he replied. "What did you expect me to do? I was a beaten docket. I'd no choice. Like, I'll still see the kids during the summer. They're going to come back to stay with her Ma and our ones will bring them up to see me. They'll probably have wee English accents by then. Who'd have thought it would turn out like this? Poor Sinead; poor kids. Poor me," he gave a false little smile and then stood up.

146

"It's a hard oul' station." He smiled again, a wee, sorry smile.

"C'mon and let's go for a walk. It's no use the two of us going into a big D. I'll be all right, I'm glad I got talking to somebody about it. You're the first one I've talked to except for Sinead. Just shows you the type of relationships we have in here. By the way, don't say anything to Egbert or Cedric. I'll tell them the morra."

We pulled the door of the study hut shut behind us. It was a bright, starlit night. We paused, hesitating, unsure of ourselves.

"Are you sure she's going to go away?" I asked, more for something to say than anything else.

"Her plane left Aldergrove ten minutes ago," Your Man answered, with a touch of impatience creeping into his voice.

"I'm sorry," I said, "I didn't mean to annoy you asking stupid questions."

"It's OK. It's not your fault. It's nobody's fault. It's just the way the cookie crumbles, as my Da used to say. The only problem is . . . "

He started to walk. I fell in alongside him.

"The only problem is, old comrade, that I love Sinead and Sinead still loves me."

He stopped in mid-stride and for the first time he looked me in the eyes. "You don't understand that, do you?"

I said nothing.

"Well, maybe you're right," he continued, "I don't understand it either. But that's what I believe and I'm going to keep believing it," he asserted determinedly, "until I'm able to come to terms with this mess. Then I'll probably be ready to believe something else. OK? But not before that. OK?"

"OK," I replied.

We walked in silence.

"You know why I need to believe that?" he asked after a short while. "You know why?" He continued without waiting for an answer. "Because in this place," he waved his hand expansively at the maze of wire and lights and watch-towers which surrounded us, "in this place you need to believe in something and right at this minute I don't have a lot to believe in. But I believe Sinead loves me."

He glared fiercely at me. Tears of anger and frustration and sorrow welled up again in his eyes.

"She just couldn't take it. And that's not her fault. OK?"

"OK, old friend," I said quietly.

"You know something else?" he asked.

"What?"

"I'm fucked." His voice finally broke. "OK?"

"OK," I replied.

I didn't look at him. I didn't need to. I knew he was crying. Not the body-wracking, sobbing convulsions of uncontrolled and disbelieving grief; no, Your Man's tears were the silent, proud and dignified longing for a lost love. He was almost regal in his sorrow.

He didn't look at me. He didn't need to. He knew I cried with him, sad little tears of solidarity and love. No one in Long Kesh saw us weeping that night as we journeyed slowly around the yard. Or if they did we didn't notice them. We were impervious to our surroundings.

We thought only, each in our different way, of Sinead and the two kids, flying high over the Irish Sea. Your Man never mentioned her to me again, not for about two years. And she never came back.

NOLLAIG SHONA DHAOIBH

"Nollaig shona dhaoibh – Happy Christmas to you all," I shout cheerfully to the silent hut. "Ho ho ho."

"This will be my fourth Christmas in jail," Your Man replies. "Four bloody Christmases in Long Kesh."

"That's not counting the two you spent in Cork," I suggest.

"I only went to Cork to order the likes of you home again," he retorts in righteous anger at myself and my smirk. "You know," he continues, "the quietness of this hut would drive you to distraction. It's like a morgue."

And so it is.

"I'm going out for a few laps of the yard. Do you fancy coming?" I ask.

"I'll catch up. G'wan ahead with Egbert and Cedric."

"We'll catch up as well," Egbert says. "We'll not be long finishing this."

He and Cedric are putting the finishing touches to a cot for Egbert's wee girl. They have already finished one for Cedric's niece.

"You shouldn't be doing that in the hut anyway," I scold in mock concern. "We've to live here. Youse have it like a bloody kip."

"It's Christmas," Cedric snaps. "Do your whack would you, like a good man. You wouldn't deprive a wee child of a cot for her doll. Would you?"

"You know me," I say. "You always play on my kind-heartedness. See youse outside?"

"We won't be long."

Outside it is cold. The camp is almost deserted. In our cage only Gerry Rooney, Tomboy, wee Dickie and big Sid are walking around the yard. They abuse me cheerfully for being on my own. In the study hut Bik and Bobby Sands practise for the Christmas concert. I lean against the door and listen as their guitar-picking stops and Bobby's clear voice rises in "Silent Night".

Óiche chiúin, óiche Mhic Dé

Cách in suan, dís araon

Dís is dílse's faire le spéis

Naíon beag groígheal

Ceannann tais caomh

Críost ina chodladh go séimh

Críost ina chodladh go séimh.

Last night, about this time, four swans flew overhead and off across there into the sunset. Me and Your Man were walking around the yard on our own. A comrade, Madra Rua, was feeding the seagulls in Cage Ten and Egbert and Cedric had left one of their cots, freshly painted, outside in the cage to dry. It was a strange scene with dusk setting in and the sun going down, giving a grey coldness to the cage lights. The seagulls, with their hysterical keening, were kiting in from the burnhouse to gobble up a late snack, and the child's cot, white and silent, stood alone on the black tarmac. Screw watch-towers, straddling the gaps between the cages, looked down their noses at us and then, as the last of its colours drained from the sun, after a magic moment of complete silence we heard the heavy beating of wings and the swans passed overhead in single file, chasing the sun as it retreated before them.

This evening ice covers the yard, icicles hang from the huts and the frost has built its own venetian blinds on the wire. They turn the fences into dull grey shimmering walls. Looking straight at the wire you can see just one expanse of optical wall. Looking at it from the side, through the shutters of ice, the football-pitch with its watch-towers comes into focus. At the front gate a robin flaunts its red breast and a pair of pied wagtails patrol their territory between the cages. Screws wrapped in their winter greatcoats huddle in watch-towers, miserable reflections of all they survey.

To my left the searchlights above the H-Blocks crane high over us all. In cells young POWs can be found, sitting or lying on the floor, always in the corner. At half past seven this morning breakfast was left in . . .

> The cell door opens to let fresh air in.
> Everyone raises his head for a look at the sky.
> Free spirits haunting the sky of liberty,
> Do you know your own kind are languishing in
>   prison?

That's how Ho Chi Minh describes it in his *Prison Diary*. Some things are universal. In the H-Blocks the POW sits, wrapped in a blanket, as far from the pisspot of stale urine as the small cell permits, and eats the mush from the tray.

Last year Republican prisoners in the Crum, Armagh, Long Kesh, Magilligan, Portlaoise, The Curragh, Mountjoy and Limerick prepared for Christmas.

Last year in Hull, Wormwood Scrubs, Wakefield, Albany, Strangeways, Long Lartin, Gartree, Winchester, Winston Green, Parkhurst, Durham, Walton Leicester, Bristol, Aylesbury and Perth, Republican prisoners made ready for the festive season. This year they prepare themselves once more. It is the same in other struggles. For a Vietnamese in jail in Southern China ...

> In the cold autumn night, without mattress, without
>   blankets,
> Lying with back curled round and legs folded up
>   close,
> I try in vain to sleep. The moonlight on the plantains
> Increases the sense of cold, and through the window-
>   bars
> The Great Bear draws up alongside and looks in.

In homes throughout Ireland and England families await the coming of Christ's birthday. In many homes Christmas this year will be a mere memory of Christmases long gone. A home is a family. In jail the family, the home is a memory.

With only memories to sustain it, Christmas is a lonely time. But then, memories keep us together. Memories of the past provide us with the determination needed to endure the present and to be ready for the future.

Kieran Nugent is four months in solitary wrapped in a blanket. No Christmas cards, holly, mistletoe or turkey. No tinsel or Christmas tree. Santa Claus is forbidden to visit prisoners. The materialistic side of Christmas is locked out. But a finer thing, a better thing, a holier thing is locked in. In cells everywhere the spirit of Christmas is imprisoned.

I sigh loudly. Bik opens the study-hut door. The sudden noise shakes me from my musings. He and Bobby step into the yard.

They also cheerfully abuse me.

"Did the boys finally break you?"

"I can't do a minute of it," I reply.

They laugh and go into their huts. I stomp the coldness out of my feet and walk out into the centre of the cage. Leaning my head back I gaze skywards. I can see forever. The inky black heavens with thousands of pinpricking Bethlehem stars stretches into eternity. I think of a different festival, in a different country, to another poem of Ho Chi Minh.

> In jail we also celebrate the mid-autumn festival
> For us the autumn moon and wind bear a flavour of sadness
> Being deprived of freedom to enjoy the autumn moon
> My heart wanders after her on her course across the sky.

"His neck is sore." It is Egbert, Cedric and Your Man trooping out of the hut and descending upon me.

"What?" I ask, a little startled.

"I was just saying it's your sore neck has you standing like that."

"Nawh, my neck isn't sore. I was just thinking."

"Ach, you don't expect us to believe that, you dunderhead. To think you have to have a brain."

"OK, OK, let's just go for a good boul. I need a long walk."

"He's broke," they chortle.

"Like a plate," Egbert laughs.

"What were you thinking about?"

"Mostly about Christmas and poetry. I'm reading a book of Ho Chi Minh's prison poetry. And I was thinking of Christmas and of all the people in prison here, in South Africa, in Britain, all over the world." We walk slowly around the yard, four abreast.

"Walls and bars do not a prison make," Your Man volunteers.

"They bloody well help," says Cedric.

"Prison is meant to break our spirits. The system aims to exploit human weakness. It is punitive. It is geared to institutionalizing us, to killing our individuality," Egbert intones.

Cedric scoffs. "Plenty of big words! You must have swallowed a dictionary."

"I'm only saying that prison cannot contain the mind which wishes to be free, which refuses to be contained."

"Ach, c'mon lads," Your Man says. "Let's not get too heavy. It's not the end of the world. It's Christmas. Give's a hug."

He grabs us and we wrestle into a rowdy scrum, pushing, pulling and horse-playing, yahoo-ing and yelling together.

"That's better," Cedric gasps as we separate. We all breathe heavily, faces rosy and eyes bright from our exertions.

"Let's go in for a mug of tea," I suggest, my melancholy exorcised.

"Whoah, hold on to your horses. Here's the Madra. It's feeding time at the zoo."

We stop at the wire and look over towards Cage Ten as Madra Rua pulls his box of dinner scraps into the yard.

"Nollaig shona dhuit!" we yell at him.

"Youse are in great form," he shouts. "Nollaig shona dhaoibh!"

We watch as he waits for the seagulls to arrive. They wheel in as if by appointment, squealing and screeching in great flocks, one hundred or maybe two hundred birds. It reminds you of Bangor, Ardglass or, in a place like this, of the tiphead at Duncrue Street. The odd pair of rooks flap in among the seagulls, and from his vantage point on the cage fence a solitary grey hooded crow glares disdainfully at his ill-mannered relations.

"How long has he been doing that?" Your Man asks.

"Too long," Cedric tells him.

"Since the Pope was an altar boy," says Egbert.

"There's not many of us left," he shouts to Madra.

Madra waves back. He finishes feeding his birds. A young seagull greedier than his fellows kites in for a final morsel. He strikes the top wires, panics, and falls screeching into coils of razor wire. A quick, hysterical flutter and he is caught fast, wings hooked to the barbs. Tiny flakes of ice dislodge and spiral to the ground. The seagull thrashes about, regurgitates, and tiny specks of red blood stain his breast.

An Madra Rua approaches. He goes off and returns with a table. A younger comrade follows close behind with a chair and together they erect a makeshift platform. The younger man scrambles on top. The seagull lunges at him. They fight a short duel. Madra holds the shaking table and gives advice. The seagull quietens. The young man grips its neck and pulls a wing free. I can see the razor wire resisting, the barb tearing flesh, the seagull struggling again. One final tug and it is free, hanging unceremoniously at arm's length. Then a slow, clumsy flop to the ground.

We cheer. Your Man kicks and punches the wire in applause.

"Well done, Madra. Youse are brilliant!" We shout to him and his comrade.

Madra gives us a cheerful thumbs-up salute. His friend shouts a Christmas greeting. Madra waves his arms at the gull. It rises hesitantly from the yard and flies off slowly and awkwardly. It clears the fences. We watch as it disappears limpingly over the H-Blocks, past the British Army watch-tower, out of sight and into freedom.

All is quiet once again. Your Man and Cedric and Egbert and I continue to walk our time slowly around the yard of Cage Eleven. We think of our families and of friends and foes and uninvolved, who will endure a lonely Christmas because they have lost loved ones in the Irish struggle. Our thoughts are also with the women in Armagh and the men in the H-Blocks, naked and in solitary.

We retire to the hut just before lock-up. Your Man and Egbert make the tea. Cedric and I butter some bread. Your Man hands around the snout.

"Don't say I didn't give you anything for Christmas," he says.

"Give my head peace," Cedric replies, as he rolls smokes for us all. "Do you want to hear a poem?"

"Nawh," we chorus.

"Well you're going to," he tells us, clearing his throat.

"Yule logs spreading warmth,
Light reflected on cheering glass;
Jesus, how humanity has died,
Indifference nailed it to a cross.

"What do youse think of that?"

We ignore him.

"I said what d'youse think of that?"

"It's really Christmassy," says Your Man. "Just what we need to cheer us up."

"I prefer something more festive," I mutter.

"I'm dreaming of a white Christmas," Egbert croons.

"Rudolph the red-nosed reindeer," jingles Your Man.

"Ach, shut up," Cedric grins. "Do your whack would youse."

"You do your whack!" we bellow at him.

Outside it starts to snow. Cage Eleven of Long Kesh settles uneasily into its wintering over Christmas. The Hut OC turns off the lights. The hut is bathed in an orange glow from the lights outside on the perimeter fence. Snowflakes swirl against the windows. The wind howls through the wire.

"Óiche mhaith, muckers," Egbert shouts from below his blankets.

"Onward to freedom," Your Man replies. "Tiocfaidh ár lá," he yells.

"Nollaig shona dhaoibh," says Cedric. "Nollaig shona dhaoibh, comrades."

"Nollaig shona," we reply.

THE POLITICS OF IRISH FREEDOM
Gerry Adams

"Adams' 'personal statement' must rank as the most considerable one to date from a leading member of the republican movement clarifying and defending its aims and methods. It thus has a role to play as one corrective among others to the flow of misinformation that passes for journalistic analysis of affairs in the North of Ireland, both in Britain and the Republic." *New Statesman*

"Gerry Adams' book will help clear the deck of many popular but outdated stereotypes of the Provisionals." *Fortnight*

"Adams writes well, with a combination of cool-headedness and passion, and next to no vituperation." *Sunday Tribune*

"A highly personal and readable account of the struggle to achieve an independent united Ireland." *City Limits*

"It is a succinct and readable restatement of the republican position." *Irish Political Studies*

"Essential reading, both for people needing an introduction to Irish politics and for people who think they know it all." *Leeds Other Paper*

"A very readable and important book." *Irish Democrat*

"The most coherent description yet of the new Provos." *Phoenix*

Paperback £4.95

SECOND–CLASS TAXI
Sylvester Stein

"The first satirical novel written about apartheid . . . a great book." *Cape Argus*

"Both comical and sad . . . well worth reading for a lighter look at the whole situation." *Anti-Apartheid News*

"Very funny . . . a delight to read." *Rand Daily Mail*

"The first and one of the best satirical novels about the daftness and the pain of apartheid . . . clothed in a robust Dickensian humour that stretches from savagery to affection." *Guardian* (London)

"The satire is quite outstandingly brilliant." *News Letter* (Belfast)

"In face of all the strong feelings about apartheid, it is a daring experiment to try to be funny about it, but this book succeeds." *Glasgow Herald*

"You will remember this book when many more serious ones on the subject are forgotten." Elizabeth Bowen, *The Tatler*

Paperback £4.95

TWENTY YEARS ON
Edited by Michael Farrell

"Powerful collection from nine participants in the stormy birth of the civil rights movement in the north of Ireland." *Socialist Outlook*

"Vividly recaptures the revolutionary spirit of the 1960s." *USI News*

"The quality of the essays is first rate." *Tribune*

Paperback £4.95

BELFAST: CITY OF SONG
Maurice Leyden

"These songs spring from the streets and lanes of Belfast; they are redolent of the mill stack, the shipyard gantry, the square sett and the redbrick terrace." David Hammond

"A book of major importance to the student of Belfast history." *Belfast Telegraph*

"This is one of the best books of its kind." *Belfast News Letter*

Paperback £8.95

THE CHRISTY MOORE SONGBOOK
Edited by Frank Connolly
with an Introduction by Donal Lunny

Over a hundred songs with music. Each song is accompanied by a short note by Christy, and the book is illustrated with photographs. The only songbook ever to reach the Number One in the book bestseller lists, *The Christy Moore Songbook* has established itself as a perennial favourite amongst followers of the song tradition.

Paperback £4.95